THE ISLAND QUEEN

R. M. BALLANTYNE

1st WORLD
LIBRARY
Literary Society

The Island Queen

R. M. Ballantyne

© 1st World Library, 2007
PO Box 2211
Fairfield, IA 52556
www.1stworldlibrary.com
First Edition

LCCN: 2007934206

Softcover ISBN: 978-1-4218-9676-2
Hardcover ISBN: 978-1-4218-9776-9
eBook ISBN: 978-1-4218-9576-5

Purchase *"The Island Queen"*
as a traditional bound book at:
www.1stWorldLibrary.com/purchase.asp?ISBN=978-1-4218-9676-2

1st World Library is a literary, educational organization
dedicated to:

- Creating a free internet library of downloadable ebooks

- Hosting writing competitions and offering book publishing scholarships.

Interested in more 1st World Library books? contact:
literacy@1stworldlibrary.com
Check us out at: www.1stworldlibrary.com

1st World Library Literary Society

Giving Back to the World

"If you want to work on the core problem, it's early school literacy."

- James Barksdale, former CEO of Netscape

"No skill is more crucial to the future of a child, or to a democratic and prosperous society, than literacy."

- Los Angeles Times

"Literacy... means far more than learning how to read and write... The aim is to transmit... knowledge and promote social participation."

- UNESCO

"Literacy is not a luxury, it is a right and a responsibility. If our world is to meet the challenges of the twenty-first century we must harness the energy and creativity of all our citizens."

- President Bill Clinton

"Parents should be encouraged to read to their children, and teachers should be equipped with all available techniques for teaching literacy, so the varying needs and capacities of individual kids can be taken into account."

- Hugh Mackay

CHAPTER ONE

DETHRONED BY FIRE AND WATER—
A TALE OF THE SOUTHERN HEMISPHERE

THE OPEN BOAT

Early one morning, in the year 18 hundred and something, the great Southern Ocean was in one of its calmest moods, insomuch that the cloudlets in the blue vault above were reflected with almost perfect fidelity in the blue hemisphere below, and it was barely possible to discern the dividing-line between water and sky.

The only objects within the circle of the horizon that presented the appearance of solidity were an albatross sailing in the air, and a little boat floating on the sea.

The boat rested on its own reflected image, almost motionless, save when a slight undulation of the water caused the lower edge of its reflection to break off in oily patches; but there was no dip of oars at its sides, no rowers on its thwarts, no guiding hand at the helm.

Evidently the albatross regarded the boat with curiosity not unmixed with suspicion, for it sailed in wide circles round it, with outstretched neck, head turned on one side, and an eye bent inquiringly downward. By slow degrees the circles diminished, until the giant bird floated almost directly over the boat. Then, apparently, it saw more than enough to satisfy its curiosity, for, uttering a hoarse cry, it swooped aside, and, with a flap of its mighty wings, made off towards the horizon, where it finally disappeared.

The flap and the cry seemed, however, to have put life into the little boat, for a human head rose slowly above the gunwale. It was that of a youth, of about twenty years of age, apparently in the last stage of exhaustion. He looked round slowly, with a dazed expression, like one who only half awakes from sleep. Drawing his hand across his brow, and gazing wistfully on the calm sea, he rose on his knees with difficulty, and rested his arms on a thwart, while he turned his gaze with a look of intense anxiety on the countenance of a young girl who lay in the bottom of the boat close beside him, asleep or dead.

"It looks like death," murmured the youth, as he bent over the pale face, his expression betraying sudden alarm; "and it must—it must come to this soon; yet I cannot bear the thought. O God, spare her!"

It seemed as if the prayer were answered at once, for a fluttering sigh escaped from the girl's bloodless lips, but she did not awake.

"Ah! sleep on, dear sister," said the youth, "it is all the comfort that is left to you now. Oh for food! How often I have wasted it; thought lightly of it; grumbled because it was not quite to my taste! What would I not give for a little of it now—a very little!"

He turned his head away from the sleeping girl, and a wolfish glare seemed to shoot from his eyes as they rested on

R. M. Ballantyne

something which lay in the stern of the boat.

There were other human beings in that boat besides the youth and his sister—some still living, some dead, for they had been many days on short allowance, and the last four days in a state of absolute starvation—all, save Pauline Rigonda and her little brother Otto, whose fair curly head rested on his sister's arm.

During the last two nights, when all was still, and the starving sailors were slumbering, or attempting to slumber, Dominick Rigonda—the youth whom we have just introduced to the reader—had placed a small quantity of broken biscuit in the hands of his sister and little brother, with a stern though whispered command to eat it secretly and in silence.

Obediently they ate, or rather devoured, their small portion, wondering where their brother had found it. Perchance they might have relished it less if they had known that Dominick had saved it off his own too scant allowance, when he saw that the little store in the boat was drawing to an end—saved it in the hope of being able to prolong the lives of Pauline and Otto.

This reserve, however, had been also exhausted, and it seemed as if the last ray of hope had vanished from Dominick's breast, on the calm morning on which our tale opens.

As we have said, the youth glared at something lying in the stern of the boat. It was a tarpaulin, which covered a human form. Dominick knew that it was a dead body—that of the cabin-boy, who had died during the night with his head resting on Dominick's arm. The two men who lay sleeping in the bow knew nothing of his death, and they were so weak from exhaustion at the time the boy died that Dominick had thought it unnecessary to rouse them. The poor boy's emaciated frame could lie till morning, he thought, and then the sleepers would assist him to put it gently into the sea.

But when morning came, the pangs of hunger assailed the self-denying youth with terrible power, and a horrible thought occurred to him. He opened a large clasp-knife, and, creeping towards the body, removed the tarpaulin. A faint smile rested on the dead lips—the same smile that had moved them when Dominick promised to carry the boy's last loving message to his mother if he should survive.

He dropped the knife with a convulsive shudder, and turned his eyes on his sleeping sister and brother. Then he thought, as he picked up the knife again, how small an amount of food would suffice to keep these two alive for a few days longer, and surely a sail *must* come in sight at last; they had waited for it, expectingly, so long!

Suddenly the youth flung the knife away from him with violence, and endeavoured with all his might to lift the body of the boy. In the days of his strength he could have raised it with one hand. Now he strove and energised for many minutes, before he succeeded in raising it to the gunwale. At last, with a mighty effort, he thrust it overboard, and it fell into the sea with a heavy plunge.

The noise aroused the two men in the bow, who raised themselves feebly. It was to them an all too familiar sound. Day by day they had heard it, as one and another of their comrades had been committed to the deep. One of the men managed to stand up, but as he swayed about and gazed at Dominick inquiringly, he lost his balance, and, being too weak to recover himself, fell over the side. He reappeared for a moment with outstretched arms and hands clutching towards the boat. Then he sank, to be seen no more. The other man, who had been his intimate friend and messmate, made a frantic effort to save him. His failure to do so seemed to be more than the poor fellow could bear, for he sprang up with the wild laugh and the sudden strength of a maniac, and leaped into the sea.

Dominick could do nothing to prevent this. While staring at the little patch of foam where the two men had gone down, he was startled by the sound of his sister's voice.

"Are they *all* gone, brother?" she asked, in a low, horrified tone.

"All—all, sister. Only you, and Otto, and I left. How soundly the poor boy sleeps!"

"I wish it might please God to let him die thus," said Pauline, with a weary sigh that told eloquently of hope deferred.

"Your wish may be granted," returned Dominick, "for the dear boy seems to be sinking. It can scarcely, I think, be natural sleep that prevented the shout of that poor fellow from arousing him. But lie down again, Pauline; sleep may do you a little good if you can obtain it, and I will watch."

"And pray," suggested the poor girl, as she lay down again, languidly.

"Yes, I will pray. Surely a sail must appear soon!"

Dominick Rigonda was strong in youthful hope even in that hour of sorest trial, but he was not strong in faith. He prayed, however, and found his faith strengthened in the act, for he looked up immediately after with a feeling amounting almost to certainty, that the long-expected and wished-for sail would greet his eyes. But no sail was visible in all the unbroken circle of his horizon. Still the faith which had prompted the eager gaze did not quite evaporate. After the first shock of disappointment at his prayer not being answered according to its tenor, his assurance that God would yet send relief returned in some degree, and he was not altogether disappointed, though the answer came at last in a way that he did not expect.

After sitting in a half-sleeping condition for some time, he aroused himself, and crept with considerable difficulty to the bow to procure the blanket which had covered the two men who had just perished. A corner of the blanket had caught on the end of one of the floor-planks. In disengaging it Dominick chanced to raise the plank which was loose, and observed something like a bundle lying underneath. Curiosity prompted him to examine it. He found that it was wrapped in canvas, and carefully tied with cord. Opening it he discovered to his surprise and intense joy that it contained some ship's biscuit, a piece of boiled pork, and a flask of water.

Only those who have been suddenly presented with food and drink, while starving can appreciate the feelings that filled the heart of the poor youth with laughter and thanksgiving; but his joy was not selfish, for the prospect of immediate personal relief had but a secondary place in his thoughts.

Hastening with the inestimable treasure to the place where his brother and sister lay, he carefully spread it out on a piece of sailcloth, and cut a few thin slices of the pork before arousing them.

"Awake, sister, and eat!" he said at last, gently shaking Pauline by the shoulder.

"O Dominick!" she exclaimed, raising herself, and gazing eagerly at the food. "I was dreaming of this when you awoke me!"

R. M. Ballantyne

"That's odd, now," said little Otto, who had also been aroused, "for I was dreaming of eating! And I am so hung—"

He got no further, for, having clutched a handful of biscuit, he suddenly stopped the way of utterance.

"How good of you, Dom!" said Pauline, eating with as much relish, though not with such voracity, as her little brother, "Where did you get this?"

"No matter; eat and be thankful," said Dominick curtly, for he was himself eating with wolfish haste by that time. He restrained himself, however, after a few minutes.

"Hold! We must not indulge too freely. It will hurt us after fasting so long. Besides, this supply is very small, and must be made to last as long as possible. No, my boy, you must eat no more at this time, but you may drink a little."

About a table-spoonful of water was measured out to each, and then the remainder of the food was carefully wrapped up and put away.

"Do you think that this supply was hidden by one of the poor fellows who left us this morning?" asked Pauline.

"I think so; and no doubt his motive was a good one. You know he was very fond of his messmate. I should think he saved up his allowance to help him; but, whatever the motive, it has proved a blessing to us—"

He ceased speaking, for both sister and little brother had drooped their weary heads, and were again in a heavy slumber. Dominick himself felt intensely the desire to follow their example, but he resisted it, feeling that it was his duty to watch for the long-expected sail that never appeared. At first his efforts were successful, but by degrees the tendency to sleep became so overpowering that his struggles were unavailing. Sense of duty and every other motive gave way before it; his head finally dropped forward, and, with a heavy sigh of contentment, he followed his brother and sister to the land of Nod.

Profound, prolonged, and refreshing was that sweet slumber, after the first good meal these poor castaways had eaten for many days. The weather fortunately continued bright and warm, so that they did not suffer so much from exposure as on previous days, and the gentle rocking of the boat tended to deepen and prolong their repose.

Thus they floated peacefully during the greater part of that day—the one solitary speck on the surface of the great ocean, for the albatross seemed to have finally forsaken them.

Towards noon a light westerly breeze sprang up. It was not sufficient to raise a sea or disturb the sleepers, but, in conjunction with ocean currents, it drifted them to the south-east at a considerable rate, so that in the evening, without the aid of oar or sail, they were far from the spot upon the sea where we introduced them to the reader.

At last Dominick awoke with a long-drawn sigh, and, raising his head, looked over the side of the boat. An exclamation of surprise and joy broke from him, for there, like a speck, where something like a heavy bank of clouds rested on the horizon, was the long-expected sail.

His first impulse was to awaken the sleepers, but he checked himself. He would look more carefully. His eyes might be deceiving him, and the disappointment, if he should be mistaken, would be overwhelming. He would spare them that. Rising to his feet he shaded his eyes with one hand, and gazed long and earnestly.

The longer he looked, however, and the more he rubbed his eyes, the more convinced was he that a vessel was really in sight.

"Pauline," he said at length, with suppressed emotion, as he gently shook her arm, "see, God *has* answered our prayers: a vessel is in sight!"

The poor girl raised herself quickly, with an exclamation of thankfulness, and gazed intently in the direction pointed out.

"It is, surely it is a ship," she said, "but—but—don't you think there is something curious about its appearance?"

"I have indeed been puzzled during the last few minutes," replied Dominick. "It seems as if there were something strange under her, and her position, too, is rather odd.—Ho! Otto, rouse up, my boy, and look at the vessel coming to save us. Your eyes are sharp! Say, d'you see anything strange about her?"

Thus appealed to, Otto, who felt greatly refreshed by his good meal and long sleep, sat up and also gazed at the vessel in question.

"No, Dom," he said at length; "I don't see much the matter with her, except that she leans over on one side a good deal, and there's something black under and around her."

"Can it be a squall that has struck her?" said Pauline. "Squalls, you know, make ships lie over very much at times, and cause the sea round them to look very dark."

"It may be so," returned Dominick doubtfully. "But we shall

soon see, for a squall won't take very long to bring her down to us."

They watched the approaching vessel with intense eagerness, but did not again speak for a considerable time. Anxiety and doubt kept them silent. There was the danger that the vessel might fail to observe them, and as their oars had been washed away they had no means of hoisting a flag of distress. Then there was the unaccountable something about the vessel's appearance, which puzzled and filled them with uncertainty. At last they drew so near that Dominick became all too well aware of what it was, and a sinking of the heart kept him still silent for a time.

"Brother," said Pauline at last in a sad voice, as she turned her dark eyes on Dominick, "I fear it is only a wreck."

"You are right," he replied gloomily; "a wreck on a barren shore, too. Not a scrap of vegetation on it, as far as I can see—a mere sandbank. Currents are carrying us towards it, and have led us to fancy that the vessel was moving."

He spoke with bitterness, for the disappointment was very great, and physical weakness had rendered him less able to bear it than he might otherwise have been.

"Don't get grumpy, Dom," said Otto, with a slightly humorous look that was peculiar to him—a look which had not lighted up his eyes for many days past.

"I *won't* get grumpy," returned Dominick with sudden energy, patting the boy's head. "It is quite clear that a good feed and a long rest were all you required to set up your plucky little spirit again."

"Dom," said Pauline, who had been looking intently at the

wreck, "is there not something like a line of white close to the wreck?"

"Ay, there is," replied Dominick, his countenance again becoming grave; "it is a line of breakers, through which it will be very difficult to steer our little boat."

"Steer, Dom," exclaimed Otto, with a look of surprise; "how can you talk of steering at all, without oar or helm?"

"I must make one of the floor-planks do for both," returned Dominick.

"I say," continued the boy, "I'm horribly hungry. Mayn't I have just a bite or two more?"

"Stay, I'm thinking," replied the other.

"Think fast then, please, for the wolf inside of me is howling."

The result of Dominick's thinking was that he resolved to consume as much of their stock of provisions as possible in one meal, in order to secure all the strength that was available by such means, and thus fit them for the coming struggle with the surf. "For," said he, "if we get capsized far from the shore, we have no chance of reaching it by swimming in our present weak condition. Our only plan is to get up all the strength we can by means of food. So here goes!"

He untied the bundle as he spoke, and spread the contents on his knees. Otto—who was, indeed, a plucky little fellow, and either did not realise or did not fear the danger that lay before him—commenced to eat with almost jovial avidity. Indeed, all three showed that they had benefited greatly by what they had already eaten, and now, for the first time during many days, consumed what they considered a full and satisfactory meal, while they drifted slowly, but steadily, towards the land.

As they neared it, the heavy mass on the horizon, which they had taken for a bank of clouds, became more distinct. A light haze cleared away and showed it to be an island, to which the sandbank formed a barrier reef; but any interest that might have been aroused by this discovery was absorbed by present anxiety, for the white and gleaming surf warned them that a serious and critical moment in their lives was fast approaching. Pauline was awed into silence, and even Otto's countenance became gradually solemnised.

CHAPTER TWO

WRECKED ON A REEF

The coral reefs, which in various shapes and sizes stud the Southern seas, are sometimes rendered almost unapproachable by the immense waves which fall upon them. Even in the calmest weather these huge breakers may be seen falling with prolonged roar on the beach. The lightest undulation on the sea, which might almost escape observation away from land, takes the form of a grand, quiet billow as it draws near to an islet or reef, and finally, coming majestically on, like a wall of rolling crystal, breaks the silence suddenly by its thunderous fall, and gives to the sands a temporary fringe of pure white foam.

To ride in on the crest of one such roller on a piece of board and leap upon the shore, is a feat peculiar to South Sea islanders, who are trained to the water from earliest infancy. To do the same thing in a small boat, without oars, without strength, without experience, almost without courage, is a feat that no South Sea islander would attempt, and the necessity for performing which might cause the hair of any islander's head to stand on end.

That Dominick Rigonda's hair did not stand on end, as he sat there with pale cheeks and compressed lips, was probably due to the fact that he had thrust his straw hat tightly down on his brows.

As the boat drew nearer to the reef, both Pauline and Otto had risen, in the strength of their hearty meal, and were now seated on the thwarts of the boat. Their brother had selected the thickest floor-plank, and cut it roughly into the form of an oar with a clasp-knife. He now sat with it over the stern, sculling gently—very gently, however, for he reserved the little strength that remained to him for the critical moment.

The undulations of the sea, which had rocked them hitherto so softly, had by that time assumed a decided form and force, so that the boat rose on the oily back of each billow that passed under it, and slid back into a watery hollow, to be relifted by each successive wave.

"You look very anxious," said Pauline, clasping her hands on her knee, and gazing earnestly in her brother's face.

"I cannot help it," returned Dominick, curtly.

"Is our danger then so great?"

Dominick only half admitted that it was. He did not wish to alarm her, and tried to smile as he said that the struggle would be brief—it would soon be over.

"But tell me, where lies the danger?" persisted Pauline. "I do not quite see it."

"'Where ignorance is bliss,' dear, 'tis folly to be wise,'" returned Dominick, with an unsuccessful effort to look more at ease.

"Nay, brother, but I am not ignorant that danger exists—only

R. M. Ballantyne

ignorant as to the amount and nature of it. Surely there cannot be much risk in pushing our boat through that white foam that lines the shore with so soft a fringe."

"I should think not," broke in the pert and inexperienced Otto; "why, Pina," (thus he abridged his sister's name), "there's as much danger, I should think, in pushing through a tub of soap-suds."

"Come, Dom," returned the girl, "explain it to me; for if you don't point out where the danger really lies, if you leave me in this state of partial ignorance, I shall be filled with alarm instead of bliss from this moment till we reach the shore."

"Well, well, sister," said Dominick, when thus urged; "if you must have it, I will explain."

He went on to show that when the boat came near the shore the waves would grasp it, instead of letting it slip back; would carry it swiftly in on their crests, so that the great difficulty in such a case would be to keep the boat's head pointing to the land, and if he failed to do so, they would infallibly be overturned and have to swim ashore.

"Well, that would be unpleasant, Dom," said the ignorant, as well as innocent, Pauline, "but it would not matter much, for we can all swim—thanks to you for insisting on teaching us long ago."

"We will try our best," said Dominick, who thereupon relapsed into silence, wisely resolving to let his sister retain all the "bliss" of "ignorance" that was possible under the circumstances.

Indeed, there was not much more time for conversation, for the power of the waves was beginning to be felt by the little craft, and the clumsy oar did not act with as much precision or force as was desirable, while Dominick's weakness rendered the steering difficult. Pauline now began to realise the danger somewhat more clearly from experience, and even Otto showed symptoms of surprise that amounted very nearly to alarm, as the boat at one point made a sudden rush on a wave-top as if it meant to try a race with it, and then as suddenly slipped back into the hollow behind, as if it had been disheartened, feeling that there was no chance.

At last they reached the point of greatest danger. The huge waves, as we have said, commenced out at sea in long, gentle undulations. Nearer the shore they advanced in the shape of glassy walls, one after another, like successive lines of indomitable infantry in time of war. Further in, the tops of these waves began to gurgle and foam, and gather real, instead of seeming, motion, as they rushed towards their fall. It was here that the boat showed symptoms of becoming unmanageable.

"Why, the water's beginning to boil!" exclaimed Otto, in some anxiety.

"Hold on, boy, and keep quiet," said his brother.

As he spoke, the water gurgled up, so that it seemed as if about to pour inboard all round. At the same time the boat made a rush shoreward as if suddenly endowed with life. Dominick struggled manfully to keep the stern to the sea. He succeeded, but in another moment the boat slipped back. It had not been fairly caught, and the wave passed on to fall with a roar like thunder a hundred yards or so ahead.

"The next will do it," said Dominick, with an anxious glance behind, where a crystal wall was coming grandly on— unnaturally high, it seemed to them, owing to their position in the hollow.

No need to tell Otto now to hold on! No need to explain difficulty or danger to Pauline! As her brother stood at the oar, quivering as much from weakness as exertion, she understood it all. But she was brave, and she could swim. This latter fact lent her additional confidence. Best of all, she had faith in God, and her spirit was calmed, for, whether life or death lay before her, she knew that her soul was "safe."

As Dominick had prophesied, the next wave took them fairly in its grasp. For a few moments the water hissed and gurgled round them. The steersman seemed to lose control for a second or two, but quickly recovered. Then there was a bound, as if the boat had been shot from a catapult, and the billow fell. A tremendous roar, tumultuous foam all round, increasing speed! The land appeared to be rushing at them, when Dominick's oar snapped suddenly, and he went overboard. A shriek from Pauline and a shout from Otto rose high above the din of raging water, as the boat broached-to and hurled its remaining occupants into the sea.

Even in that trying moment Dominick did not lose presence of mind. He could swim and dive like a water-rat. Pushing towards his brother and sister, who were heading bravely for the shore, he shouted, "Dig your fingers and toes deep into the sand, and hold on for life, if—" (he corrected himself) "*when* you gain the beach."

It was well they were forewarned, and that they were constitutionally obedient. A few minutes later, and they were all swept up high on the beach in a wilderness of foam. The return of that wilderness was like the rushing of a millrace. Sand, stones, sticks, and seaweed went back with it in dire confusion. Prone on their knees, with fingers and toes fixed, and heads down, the brothers and sister met the rush. It was almost too much for them. A moment more, and strength as well as breath would have failed; but the danger passed, and Dominick sprang to his feet.

"Up, up! and run!" he shouted, as he caught Pauline round the waist and dragged her on. Otto needed no help. They were barely in time. The succeeding wave roared after them as if maddened at having lost its prey, and the foaming water was up with them, and almost round their knees, ere its fury was quite spent.

"Safe!" exclaimed Dominick.

"Thank God!" murmured Pauline, as she sank exhausted on the sand.

Otto, who had never seen his sister in such a state before, ran to her, and, kneeling down, anxiously seized one of her hands.

"Never fear, lad," said his brother in reassuring tones, "she'll soon come round. Lend a hand to lift her."

They bore the fainting girl up the beach, and laid her on a grassy spot under a bush. And now Dominick was glad to find that he had been mistaken in supposing that the coral reef was a mere sandbank, destitute of vegetation. Indeed, before landing, he had observed that there were a few trees on the highest part of it. He now perceived that there was quite a little grove of cocoa-nut palms, with a thicket of underwood around them, which, if not extensive, was at all events comparatively dense. He pointed out the fact to Otto, who was chafing his sister's hands.

"Ay," responded Otto, "and the island on the other side must be a goodish big one, for I got a glimpse of it through the trees as we came rushing in on that monstrous wave."

In a short time Pauline recovered, and Dominick returned to the water's edge with Otto.

"Our first care must be," he said, "to save our little boat if we can, for it is the only means we have of escaping from this island."

"Escaping!" repeated Otto, in surprise. "I don't want to escape from it, Dom."

"Indeed! why not?"

"Why, because I've dreamed about being cast on a desolate island hundreds of times, and I've read about Robinson Crusoe, and all the other Crusoes, and I've longed to be cast on one, and now I am cast on one, so I don't want to escape. It'll be the greatest fun in the world. I only hope I won't wake up, as usual, to find that it's all a dream!"

Dominick laughed (not scornfully, by any means) at the boy's enthusiasm; nevertheless he had strong sympathy with him, for the period had not passed so long ago when he himself entertained a very vivid impression of the romance of such a situation, and he did not trouble his mind about the stern realities.

"I sincerely hope it may come up to your expectations, Otto, my boy; nevertheless we must secure the boat for fishing purposes, even though we don't try to escape in it."

"For fishing! why, we have neither hooks nor lines."

"True, lad; but we have got fingers and brains. It strikes me that we shall have occasion to use all our powers and possessions if we are not to starve here, for the reef seems to have very little vegetation on it, and there is sure to be a lagoon of water on the other side, separating it from the island beyond."

"I wonder if there is fresh water on the reef," said Otto, with a very sudden look of solemnity and pursing of the mouth.

"You may well ask that. I hope there is. We will go and settle the point the moment we have secured the boat, if—"

He stopped, for he saw at that moment that the sea had taken good care to secure the boat to itself as a plaything. Having dashed it into small pieces, it was by that time busily engaged in tossing these about among the foam, now hurling the splinters high upon the shore, anon sending up long watery tongues to lick them back, and then casting them under the incoming rollers, to be further reduced into what is usually styled matchwood.

There was a small bay close at hand, where the sandy beach was strewn with rocks, in which the sea appeared to play this game with unusual vigour. It was a sort of hospital for marine incurables, into which the sea cast its broken toys when tired of smashing them up, and left them there to rot.

Regarding this spot with a thoughtful look, Dominick remarked that the wreck which lay on the rocks off the tail of the island was by no means the first that had taken place there.

"And won't be the last, I fancy," said Otto.

"Probably not. Indeed, from the appearance of this bay, and the fact that an ocean current drifted us towards the spot, I should think that the island is a particularly dangerous one for vessels. But come, we'll go see how Pina gets on, and then proceed to examine our new home."

Returning to the place where Pauline had been left, they found the poor girl wringing the water out of her dress. The news of the fate of the little boat did not seem to affect her much, she did not fully appreciate the loss, and was more taken up with the idea of thankfulness for deliverance from death.

"May I not go with you?" she asked, on hearing that her brothers were going to search for water.

"Certainly. I thought you might perhaps prefer to rest, and dry your clothes in the sun," replied Dominick.

"Walking will dry them better," said Pina. "Besides, I have quite recovered."

"You're a plucky little woman," said Otto, as they set off. "Isn't it nice to be here all by ourselves, on a real uninhabited island, quite fit for Robinson himself? Who knows but we may find Friday in the bushes!"

"Wouldn't that spoil it as an uninhabited isle?"

"A little, but not much."

"The thicket is too small to contain anything with life, I fear," said Dominick, whose anxiety as to food and drink prevented his sympathising much with the small-talk of the other two. "Luckily the weather is warm," he added, "and we won't require better shelter at present than the bushes afford, unless a storm comes.—Ho what have we here?—a path!"

They had reached the entrance to the thicket, and discovered what appeared to be an opening into it, made apparently by the hand of man.

"Nothing more likely," said Pauline. "If so many wrecks have taken place here—as you seem to think—some of the crews must have landed, and perhaps lived here."

"Ay, and died here," returned Dominick, in a grave, low tone, as he pointed to a skeleton lying on a spot which had once been cleared of bushes, but so long ago that the vegetation had partially grown up again. The man whose bleached bones lay before them had evidently perished many years before. On examination, nothing was found to afford any information about him, but when they had advanced a dozen yards further they came upon six little mounds, which showed that a party—probably a wrecked crew—had sojourned there for a time, and finally perished: so far their story was clear enough. One by one they must have sunk, until the last man had lain down to die and remain unburied.

Pushing past these sad evidences of former suffering, and feeling that the same fate might await themselves, they came to a sight which tended slightly to restore their spirits. It was a pool of water of considerable size, whether a spring or a rain-pool they could not tell. Neither did they care at that time, for the sudden feeling of relieved anxiety was so great, that they ran forward, as if under one impulse, and, lying down on their breasts, took a long refreshing draught. So powerful was the influence of this refreshment and discovery on their spirits that they became totally regardless and forgetful for the moment about food—all the more that, having so recently had a good meal, they were not hungry.

"I was sure we would find water," said Otto, as they continued to explore the thicket, "and I've no doubt that we shall find yams and plantains and breadfruits, and—aren't these the sort of things that grow wild on coral islands, Dom?"

"Yes, but I fear not on such a little scrap of reef as this. However, we shall not be quite destitute, for there are cocoanuts, you see—though not many of them. Come, our prospects are brightening, and as the sun is beginning to sink, we will look out for a suitable camping-ground."

"As far away from the skeleton, please, as possible," said Otto.

"Surely you don't suppose it can hurt you?" said Pauline.

"N-no, of course not, but it would be unpleasant to have it for a bedfellow, you know; so, the further away from it the better."

As he spoke they emerged from the thicket, at the end opposite to the spot where they had entered, and had their spirits again powerfully cheered by coming suddenly into a blaze of sunshine, for the bright orb of day was descending at that side of the islet, and his red, resplendent rays were glowing on the reef and on the palm-trees.

They also came in full view of the islet beyond, which, they now perceived, was of considerable size, and covered with vegetation, but, as Dominick had suspected, separated completely from the reef or outer isle on which they stood by a deep lagoon.

"Splendid!" exclaimed Pauline.

"As I feared," muttered Dominick, "and no means of reaching it."

"Pooh! Didn't Robinson Crusoe make rafts?" said Otto; "at least if he didn't, somebody else did, and anyhow *we* can."

"Come, let us continue our walk," said Dominick. "You don't fully appreciate the loss of our boat Otto. Don't you see that, even if we do build a raft, it will at best be a clumsy thing to manage, and heavy to pull, slow to sail, and bad to steer, and if we should chance to be on it when a stiff breeze springs up from the land, we should probably be driven out to sea and lost—or separated, if Pina should chance to have been left on shore at the time."

"What a fellow you are, Dom, for supposing chances and difficulties, and fancying they cannot be overcome," returned Otto, with the pert self-sufficiency that characterised him. "For my part I rather enjoy difficulties, because of the fun of overcoming them. Don't you see, we three can make quite sure of never being separated by never going out on our raft except together, so that we shall always enjoy ourselves unitedly, or perish in company. Then we can easily get over the difficulty of being blown out to sea, by never going on the sea at all, but confining ourselves entirely to the lagoon, which is large enough for any reasonable man, and may be larger than we think, for we can't see the whole of it from where we stand. Then, as to sailing and rowing slowly, we can overcome these difficulties by not being in a hurry,—taking things easy, you know."

To this Dominick replied that there was one difficulty which his little brother, with all his wisdom and capacity, would never overcome.

"And what may that be?" demanded Otto.

"The difficulty of being unable to talk common-sense."

"True, Dom, true, that is a great difficulty," retorted the boy, with deep humility of aspect, "for a man's conversation is greatly affected by the company he keeps, and with *you* as my only male companion, I have not much to hope for in the way of example. But even that may be got the better of by holding intercourse chiefly with Pina."

"But what if I refuse to talk?" said Pauline, with a laugh.

"Then will you be all the more able to listen, sister mine, which is the most common-sense thing that you can do, except when brother Dom speaks," said the incorrigible boy.

They had seated themselves on a bank while thus conversing, and from their position could see over a considerable portion of the lagoon. Suddenly Dominick pointed to an object a long way off, which was half concealed by the shadow of an island.

"Does it not look like a canoe?" he asked eagerly.

"Can't make it out at all," said Otto, shading his eyes with his hand.

"The sun on the water dazzles one so," observed Pauline, "that it is difficult to look steadily."

In a few moments the object which had drawn their attention sailed out from under the shade of the island, and, breaking up into fragments, rose into the air, proving itself to be a flock of large aquatic birds which had been swimming in a line.

"Things are not what they seem," observed Pauline, rising and following her brothers through a little thicket.

"What a pity!" exclaimed Otto; "I was in hopes it was a

canoeful of savages. It would be such fun to have a real Friday to be our servant."

"More likely that our Friday would kill, cook, and eat us if he could," said Dominick, to the surprise of Otto, who gave it as his opinion that savages never ate men, and asked if his brother really believed that they did.

"Indeed I do. We have it recorded by all the best authorities that South Sea islanders are given to this horrible practice. There can be no doubt about it whatever, and the less we see of these fellows in our present defenceless state the better."

"How little," said Pauline, "our dear father thought when he wrote for us to go out to him in his ship, that we should be cast on an unknown island, and the ship itself go to the bottom!"

"Little indeed, and as little did poor mother dream of such a fate," returned Dominick, "when she let us all go so readily, on the understanding that we should give father no rest until we had got him to give up business, quit Java for ever, and return home."

"Dear old mother!" said Pauline, "I wish—oh! I wish so much that we had not left her, even though it was to be for only a few months. She must be *so* lonely, with no one to talk to—"

"You forget Pina."

"Forget—what?"

"The cat," returned Otto, unable to repress a smile, which rose in spite of the ready tear that dimmed his eye at the mere mention of his mother. "You know the cat is her great resource—a sort of safety-valve. Sometimes, when I've been listening to her, lying on the rug at her feet half asleep, I've heard her talk to that cat as if it really was a human being, and tell it all about her little affairs and daily troubles and worries in quite a confidential tone. I've taken it into my head that that's mother's way of thinking aloud—she thinks at the cat, for company: and to do the brute justice, it does its best to accommodate her. I've seen it sit and stare at her by the half-hour at a time, and give a little purr or a meaiow now and then as if it wanted to speak. I'm quite sure it thinks, and wonders no doubt what idle, useless work it is to click knitting-needles together by the hour."

"Dear me, Otto," said Pauline, with a laugh, "I had no idea that you could think so much about anything."

"Think!" exclaimed the boy, indignantly; "d'you suppose that it's only stern-browed, long-legged fellows like Dom there who can think? Why, I think, and think, sometimes, to such an extent that I nearly think myself inside out! But, Pina, you don't know half as much about motherkin as I do, for when *you* are with her she usually forgets *herself*, I can see, and talks only about the things that interest *you*; whereas, when there's nobody present but *me*, she counts me for nothing, and lets me do pretty much what I like—because no doubt she thinks I'll do that whether she lets me or not—but she's wrong, for I love her far more than she thinks; and then it's when I'm quiet and she forgets me, I fancy, or thinks I'm asleep, that she comes out strong at the cat."

"Darling mother!" said Pauline, musingly. "I can see her now, in my mind, with her neat black cap and smooth braided hair, and gold spectacles, as plain as if she were sitting before me."

"I'm sorry to destroy the vision, Pina, on my own account as well as yours," observed Dominick, "but it behoves us now to look for a night's lodging, for the sun is sinking fast, and it would not be pleasant to lie down on the bare ground shelterless, fine though the climate is. Come, we will return to the place where we landed, and search for a cave or a bit of overhanging rock."

The best sleeping-place that they had up to that time discovered was undoubtedly the grove in which they had found the graves of the shipwrecked crew, but, as Otto truly remarked, it would probably result in uncomfortable dreams if they were to go to sleep in a burying-ground, alongside of a skeleton.

Accordingly they returned to the beach, and sought for some time among the *debris* of the boat for anything useful that might have been washed up, but found nothing. Then they went along-shore in the direction of the wreck which had raised their hopes so high that day when first seen, but nothing suitable was discovered until they rounded a low point of rocks, when Pauline came to a sudden pause.

"Look! a golden cave!" she exclaimed, pointing eagerly to a grassy spot which was canopied by feathery palms, and half enclosed by coral rocks, where was a cavern into which the sinking sun streamed at the moment with wonderful intensity.

Their home for that night obviously lay before them, but when they entered it and sat down, their destitution became sadly apparent. No beds to spread, no food to prepare, nothing whatever to do but lie down and sleep.

"No matter, we're neither hungry nor thirsty," said Dominick, with an air of somewhat forced gaiety, "and our clothes are getting dry. Come, sister, you must be weary. Lie down at the inner side of the cave, and Otto and I, like faithful knights, will guard the entrance. I—I wish," he added, in a graver tone, and with some hesitation, "that we had a Bible, that we might read a verse or two before lying down."

"I can help you in that," said his sister, eagerly. "I have a fair memory, you know, and can repeat a good many verses."

Pauline repeated the twenty-third Psalm in a low, sweet voice. When she had finished, a sudden impulse induced Dominick, who had never prayed aloud before, to utter a brief but fervent prayer and thanksgiving. Then the three lay down in the cave, and in five minutes were sound asleep.

Thus appropriately did these castaways begin their sojourn on a spot which was destined to be their home for a long time to come.

CHAPTER THREE

EXPLORATIONS AND DISCOVERIES

As the sun had bathed the golden cave when our castaways went to sleep, so it flooded their simple dwelling when they awoke.

"Then," exclaims the intelligent reader, "the sun must have risen in the west!"

By no means, good reader. Whatever man in his wisdom, or weakness, may do or say, the great luminaries of day and night hold on the even tenor of their way unchanged. But youth is a wonderful compound of strength, hope, vitality, carelessness, and free-and-easy oblivion, and, in the unconscious exercise of the last capacity, Pauline and her brothers had slept as they lay down, without the slightest motion, all through that night, all through the gorgeous sunrise of the following morning, all through the fervid noontide and the declining day, until the setting sun again turned their resting-place into a cave of gold.

The effect upon their eyelids was such that they winked, and awoke with a mighty yawn. We speak advisedly. There were not three separate awakenings and three distinct yawns; no, the rousing of one caused the rousing of the others in succession so rapidly that the yawns, commencing with Pauline's treble, were prolonged, through Otto's tenor down to Dominick's bass, in one stupendous monotone or slide, which the last yawner terminated in a groan of contentment. Nature, during the past few days, had been doubly defrauded, and she, having now partially repaid herself, allowed her captives to go free with restored vigour. There was, however, enough of the debt still unpaid to induce a desire in the captives to return of their own accord to the prison-house of Oblivion, but the desire was frustrated by Otto, who, sitting up suddenly and blinking at the sun with owlish gravity, exclaimed—

"Well, I never! We've only slept five minutes!"

"The sun hasn't set *yet*!"

Dominick, replying with a powerful stretch and another yawn, also raised himself on one elbow and gazed solemnly in front of him. A gleam of intelligence suddenly crossed his countenance.

"Why, boy, when we went to sleep the sun was what you may call six feet above the horizon; now it is twelve feet if it is an inch, so that if it be still setting, it must be setting upwards—a phenomenon of which the records of astronomical research make no mention."

"But it *is* setting?" retorted Otto, with a puzzled look, "for I never heard of your astronomical searchers saying that they'd ever seen the sun rise in the same place where it sets."

"True, Otto, and the conclusion I am forced to is that we have slept right on from sunset to sunset."

"So, then, we've lost a day," murmured Pauline, who in an

attitude of helpless repose, had been winking with a languid expression at the luminous subject of discussion.

"Good morning, Pina," said Dominick.

"Good evening, you mean," interrupted his brother. "Well, good evening. It matters little which; how have you slept?"

"Soundly—oh, so soundly that I don't want to move."

"Well, then, don't move; I'll rise and get you some breakfast."

"Supper," interposed Otto.

"Supper be it; it matters not.—But don't say we've lost a day, sister mine. As regards time, indeed, we have; but in strength I feel that I have gained a week or more."

"Does any one know," said Otto, gazing with a perplexed expression at the sky—for he had lain back again with his hands under his head—"does any one know what day it was when we landed?"

"Thursday, I think," said Dominick.

"Oh no," exclaimed Pauline; "surely it was Wednesday or Tuesday; but the anxiety and confusion during the wreck, and our terrible sufferings afterwards in the little boat, have quite confused my mind on that point."

"Well, now, here's a pretty state of things," continued Otto, sleepily; "we've lost one day, an' we don't agree about three others, and Dom says he's gained a week! how are we ever to find out when Sunday comes, I should like to know? There's a puzzler—a reg'lar—puzzl'—puz—"

A soft snore told that "tired Nature's sweet restorer, balmy sleep," had again taken the little fellow captive, and prolonged silence on the part of the other two proved them to have gone into similar captivity. Nature had not recovered her debt in full. She was in an exacting mood, and held them fast during the whole of another night. Then she set them finally free at sunrise on the following day, when the soft yellow light streamed on surrounding land and sea, converting their sleeping-place into a silver cave by contrast.

There was no languid or yawny awakening on this occasion. Dominick sat up the instant his eyes opened, then sprang to his feet, and ran out of the cave. He was followed immediately by Otto and Pauline, the former declaring with emphasis that he felt himself to be a "new man."

"Yes, Richard's himself again," said Dominick, as he stretched himself with the energy of one who rejoices in his strength. "Now, Pina, we've got a busy day before us. We must find out what our islet contains in the way of food first, for I am ravenously hungry, and then examine its other resources. It is very beautiful. One glance suffices to tell us that. And isn't it pleasant to think that it is all our own?"

"'The earth is the Lord's, and the fulness thereof,'" said his sister, softly.

The youth's gaiety changed into a deeper and nobler feeling. He looked earnestly at Pauline for a few seconds.

"Right, Pina, right," he said. "To tell you the truth, I was half-ashamed of my feelings that time when I broke into involuntary prayer and thanksgiving. I'm ashamed now of having been ashamed. Come, sister, you shall read the Word of God from memory, and I will pray every morning and evening as long as we shall dwell here together."

That day they wandered about their islet with more of gaiety and light-heartedness than they would have experienced had they neglected, first, to give honour to God, who not only gives us all things richly to enjoy, but also the very capacity for enjoyment.

But no joy of earth is unmingled. The exploration did not result in unmitigated satisfaction, as we shall see.

Their first great object, of course, was breakfast.

"I can't ask you what you'll have, Pina. Our only dish, at least this morning," said Dominick, glancing upwards, "is—"

"Cocoa-nuts," put in Otto.

Otto was rather fond of "putting in" his word, or, as Dominick expressed it, "his oar." He was somewhat pert by nature, and not at that time greatly modified by art.

"Just so, lad," returned his brother; "and as you have a considerable spice of the monkey in you, be good enough to climb up one of these palms, and send down a few nuts."

To do Otto justice, he was quite as obliging as he was pert; but when he stood at the foot of the tall palm-tree and looked up at its thick stem, he hesitated.

"D'you know, Dom," he said, "it seems to me rather easier to talk about than to do?"

"You are not the first who has found that out," returned his brother, with a laugh. "Now, don't you know how the South Sea islanders get up the palm-trees?"

"No; never heard how."

"Why, I thought your great authority Robinson Crusoe had told you that."

"Don't think he ever referred to it. Friday may have known how, but if he did, he kept his knowledge to himself."

"I wish you two would discuss the literature of that subject some other time," said Pauline. "I'm almost sinking for want of food. Do be quick, please."

Thus urged, Dominick at once took off his neckcloth and showed his brother how, by tying his feet together with it at a sufficient distance apart, so as to permit of getting a foot on each side of the tree, the kerchief would catch on the rough bark, and so form a purchase by which he could force himself up step by step, as it were, while grasping the stem with arms and knees.

Otto was an apt scholar in most things, especially in those that required activity of body. He soon climbed the tree, and plucked and threw down half a dozen cocoa-nuts. But when these had been procured, there still remained a difficulty, for the tough outer husk of the nuts, nearly two inches thick, could not easily be cut through with a clasp-knife so as to reach that kernel, or nut, which is ordinarily presented to English eyes in fruit-shops.

"We have no axe, so must adopt the only remaining method," said Dominick.

Laying a nut on a flat rock, he seized a stone about twice the size of his own head, and, heaving it aloft, brought it down with all his force on the nut, which was considerably crushed and broken by the blow. With perseverance and the vigorous use of a clasp-knife he at last reached the interior. Thereafter, on cocoa-nut meat and cocoa-nut milk, with a draught from a pool in the thicket they partook of their first breakfast on the reef.

"Now, our first duty is to bury the skeleton," said Dominick, when the meal was concluded; "our next to examine the land; and our last to visit the wreck. I think we shall be able to do all this in one day."

Like many, perhaps we may say most, of man's estimates, Dominick's calculation was short of the mark, for the reef turned out to be considerably larger than they had at first supposed. It must be remembered that they had, up to that time, seen it only from the low level of the sea, and from that point of view it appeared to be a mere sandbank with a slight elevation in the centre, which was clothed with vegetation. But when the highest point of this elevation was gained, they discovered that it had hidden from their view not only a considerable stretch of low land which lay behind, but an extensive continuation of the lagoon, or salt-water lake, in which lay a multitude of smaller islets of varying shapes, some mere banks of sand, others with patches of vegetation in their centres, and a few with several cocoa-nut palms on them, the nucleus, probably, of future palm groves. A large island formed the background to this lovely picture, and the irregular coral reef guarded the whole from the violence of the ocean. In some places this reef rose to a considerable height above the sea-level. In others, it was so little above it that each falling breaker almost buried it in foam; but everywhere it was a sufficient protection to the lagoon, which lay calm and placid within, encircled by its snowy fringe,—the result of the watery war outside. In one spot there was a deep entrance into this beautiful haven of peace, and that chanced to be close to the golden cave, and was about fifty yards wide. At the extremity of the reef, on the other side of this opening, lay another elevated spot, similar to their own, though smaller, and with only a few palms in the centre of it. From the sea this eminence had appeared to be a continuation of the other, and it was only when they landed that the Rigondas discovered the separation caused by the channel leading into the lagoon.

"Fairyland!" exclaimed Pauline, who could scarcely contain herself with delight at the marvellous scene of beauty that had so unexpectedly burst upon their view.

"Rather a noisy and bustling fairyland too," said Otto, referring to the numerous sea-birds that inquisitively came to look at them, as well as to the other waterfowl that went about from isle to isle on whistling wings.

The boy spoke jestingly, but it was clear from his heaving chest, partially-open mouth, and glittering eyes, that his little heart was stirred to an unwonted depth of emotion.

"Alas! that we have lost our boat," exclaimed Dominick.

To this Otto replied by expressing an earnest wish that he were able to swim as well as a South Sea islander, for in that case he would launch forth and spend the remainder of that day in visiting all the islands.

"Yes; and wouldn't it be charming," responded his brother, "to pay your aquatic visits in such pleasant company as that?"

He pointed to an object, which was visible at no great distance, moving about on the surface of the glassy sea with great activity.

"What creature is that?" asked Pauline.

"It is not a creature, Pina, only part of a creature."

"You don't mean to say it's a shark!" cried Otto, with a frown.

"Indeed it is—the back-fin of one at least—and he must have heard you, for he seems impatient to join you in your little trip to the islands."

"I'll put it off to some future day, Dom. But isn't it a pity that such pretty places should be spoiled by such greedy and cruel monsters?"

"And yet they *must* have been made for some good purpose," suggested Pauline.

"I rather suspect," said Dominick, "that if game and fish only knew who shoot and catch them, and afterwards eat them, they might be inclined to call man greedy and cruel."

"But we can't help that Dom. We must live, you know."

"So says or thinks the shark, no doubt, when he swallows a man."

While the abstruse question, to which the shark had thus given rise, was being further discussed, the explorers returned to the thicket, where they buried the skeleton beside the other graves. A close search was then made for any object that might identify the unfortunates or afford some clue to their history, but nothing of the sort was found.

"Strange," muttered Dominick, on leaving the spot after completing their task. "One would have expected that, with a wrecked ship to fall back upon, they would have left behind them evidences of some sort—implements, or books, or empty beef-casks,—but there is literally nothing."

R. M. Ballantyne

"Perhaps," suggested Pauline, "the men did not belong to this wreck. They may have landed as we have done out of a small boat, and the vessel we now see may have been driven here after they were dead."

"True, Pina, it may have been so. However, the matter must remain a mystery for the present. Meanwhile we will go and explore the low land behind our reef."

"Isn't it strange, Dom, that we should become landed proprietors in this fashion?" remarked Otto, as they walked along.

"And that, too," added Pauline, "at a time when our hopes were lowest and our case most desperate."

"'Tis a magnificent estate," said Dominick, "of which we will constitute Pina the Queen, myself the Prime Minister, and Otto the army."

To this Otto objected that, as it was the business of an army to defend the people and keep them in order, there was no use for an army, seeing that there were no people; but Dominick replied that a queen and prime minister formed part of a people, and that an army was required to defend *them*.

"To keep them in order, you should say," retorted Otto, "for that will clearly be my chief duty if I accept the situation. Well, I've no objection, on the whole, to be an army; but, please, remember that in time of peace an army is expected to do no laborious work, and that at all times it is clothed and fed by the State. Now, Queen Pina the First, what would your Majesty wish the army to do?"

"Go forth and subdue the land," replied Pina the First,

promptly, with quite a regal sweep of her hand towards the low ground and the lagoon beyond.

"Will your Majesty deign to instruct me how I am to begin?"

The Queen hesitated. She was rather puzzled, as rulers sometimes are when required to tackle details.

"May it please your Majesty," said Dominick, coming to the rescue like a true premier, "it is the chief duty of a prime minister to advise his sovereign. If it be your pleasure, I would recommend that the army should be sent down into yonder clump of reeds to ascertain what revenue is to be derived from the inhabitants thereof in the shape of wildfowl, eggs, etcetera, while I visit the shore of the lagoon to ascertain the prospects of supply, in the form of shellfish, from that quarter. Meanwhile, I would further advise your Majesty to sit down on this coral throne, and enjoy the contemplation of your kingdom till we return."

With a dignified bow and a little laugh Queen Pina assented, and the Prime Minister went off to the shore, while the army defiled towards the marsh.

Left alone, Pina the First soon forgot her royal condition in contemplation of the lovely prospect before her. As she gazed over the sand, and across the lagoon, and out on the gleaming sea, her thoughts assumed the wings of the morning and flew away over the mighty ocean to old England. Sadness filled her heart, and tears her eyes, as she thought of a mild little mother who had, since the departure of her three children, been reduced for companionship to a huge household cat, and who would ere long be wondering why letters were so long of coming from the dear ones who had left her.

R. M. Ballantyne

Pauline had a vivid imagination and great power of mental abstraction. She summoned up the image of the little mother so successfully that she felt as if she actually saw her knitting her socks, sadly, with her head on one side. She even heard her address the cat (she was accustomed to address the cat when alone), and express a hope that in the course of a month or six weeks more she might expect to have news of the absent ones. And Pauline almost saw the household cat, which occupied its usual place on the table at the old lady's elbow, blink its eyes with sympathy—or indifference, she could not be quite sure which. Then Pauline's wayward thoughts took a sudden flight to the island of Java, in the China seas, where she beheld a bald little old gentleman—a merchant and a shipowner—who was also her father, and who sat reading a newspaper in his office, and was wondering why his good ship *Flying Fish*—which was bringing his children to him besides a quantity of other goods—did not make its appearance, and she plainly saw the look of disappointment as he threw the paper down, exclaiming, "Odd, very odd, but she *must* turn up soon."

Pauline saw nothing more after that for some time, because her eyes were blinded with tears.

Then Queen Pina cheered up again, for she thought that surely a ship would soon pass the island and take them off. As this last thought became more definite (for Pina was very young and hopeful) her eyes dried and permitted her to observe her kingdom more clearly.

The Prime Minister, she observed, was still busy on the shore, and, from his frequently stooping to pick up something, she argued that the affairs of State in that quarter were prospering.

Presently, from the midst of a mass of reeds not far off, there arose a shout, easily recognisable as that of the army, which was followed by cries of a stupendous, yet extremely familiar, kind. Pauline started up in considerable haste, and a moment later beheld the chief authors of the noise burst from the clump of reeds in the form of a large sow and a troop of little pigs.

They were evidently in a state of wild alarm, for, besides squealing with a degree of intensity possible only to pigs, they ran in such furious haste that they stumbled over sticks and stones in reckless confusion, scrambling to their feet again in such a hurry as to ensure repeated falls, and, generally, twirling themselves and their tails in a manner that was consistent with nothing short of raving madness.

Little wonder that those creatures acted thus, for, close on their heels, gasping and glaring, the army burst forth and fell on them—literally fell on one of them, for Otto in his anxiety to catch the hindmost pig, a remarkably small but active animal, tripped over a root just as he was about to lay hold of its little tail, and fell on the top of it with fearful violence. The mechanical pressure, combining with the creature's spiritual efforts, produced a sudden yell that threw the cries of its companions quite into the shade. It might have sufficed to blow Otto into the air. Indeed, it seemed as if some such result actually followed, for, after turning a complete somersault, the boy was on his feet again as if by magic; but so also was the little pig, which, being thus forcibly separated from its family, turned aside and made for the main thicket. To cut off its retreat, the army made a sudden flank movement, headed the enemy, grasped it by the curly tail, and sought to lift it into his arms, but the curly tail straightened out, and, being exceedingly thin as well as taper, slipped from his hand. Need we say that the little pig came to the ground with a remonstrative squeal? It also rolled over. Otto, unable to check himself, flew past. The pig rose, diverged, and resumed its headlong flight. Otto doubled, came close up again, "stooped to conquer," and was on the point of coming off victorious, when, with a final shriek of mingled rage and joy, the enemy rushed through a hole under a prickly bush, while the discomfited army plunged headlong into the same, and stuck fast.

Meanwhile the rest of the porcine family had found refuge in an almost impenetrable part of the thicket.

"Pork, your Majesty," said Otto, on returning from the field of battle, "may at all events be counted as one of the products of your dominions."

"Truly it would seem so," responded the Queen, with a laugh; "nevertheless there does not appear to be much hope of its forming a source of supply to the royal larder."

"Time will show," said Dominick, coming up at the moment; "and see, here are several kinds of shellfish, which will form a pleasant addition to our fare."

"Ay, and I saw eggs among the reeds," said Otto, "some of which—"

"Not pigs' eggs, surely?" interrupted Dominick.

"They may be so," retorted Otto; "the fact that English pigs don't lay eggs, is no argument against South Sea pigs doing so, if they choose. But, as I was about to say, your Majesty, when the Premier interrupted me—some of these eggs I gathered, and would have presented them as an offering from the army, if I had not fallen and crushed them beyond repair."

In corroboration of what he said, Otto opened his coat pocket and revealed in its depths a mass of yellow substance, and broken shells.

"Horrible!" exclaimed Pauline; "how will you ever get it cleaned?"

"By turning it inside out—thus, most gracious Queen."

He reversed the pocket as he spoke, allowing the yellow compound to drip on the ground, and thereafter wiped it with grass.

"I wouldn't have minded this loss so much," he continued, "if I had not lost that little pig. But I shall know him again when I see him, and you may depend on it that he is destined ere long to be turned into pork chops."

"Well, then, on the strength of that hope we will continue the survey of our possessions," said Dominick, leading the party still further into the low grounds.

For some time the trio wandered about without making any further discoveries of importance until they came to a thicket, somewhat similar to the one near which they had been cast on shore, but much smaller. On entering it they were startled by a loud cackling noise, accompanied by the whirring of wings.

"Sounds marvellously like domestic fowls," said Dominick, as he pushed forward. And such it turned out to be, for, on reaching an open glade in the thicket, they beheld a large flock of hens running on ahead of them, with a splendid cock bringing up the rear, which turned occasionally to cast an indignant look at the intruders.

"That accounts for your eggs, Otto," observed Pauline.

"Yes, and here are more of them," said the boy, pointing to a nest with half a dozen eggs in it, which he immediately proceeded to gather.

"It is quite evident to me," remarked Dominick, as they continued to advance, "that both the pigs and fowls must have been landed from the wreck that lies on the shore, and that, after the death of the poor fellows who escaped the sea, they went wild. Probably they have multiplied, and we may find the land well stocked."

"I hope so. Perhaps we may find some more traces of the shipwrecked crew," suggested Pauline.

Their expectations were not disappointed, for, on returning in the evening from their tour of exploration, they came on a partially cleared place in the thicket beside the golden cave, which had evidently been used as a garden. In the midst of a mass of luxuriant undergrowth, which almost smothered them, vegetables of various kinds were found growing— among others the sweet potato.

Gathering some of these, Otto declared joyfully that he meant to have a royal feast that night, but a difficulty which none of them had thought of had to be faced and overcome before that feast could be enjoyed. It was just as they arrived at the golden cave that this difficulty presented itself to their minds.

"Dom," said Otto, with a solemn look, "how are we to make a fire?"

"By kindling it, of course."

"Yes, but, you stupid Premier, where are we to find a light?"

"To tell you the truth, my boy," returned Dominick, "I never thought of that till this moment, and I can't very well see my way out of the difficulty."

Pauline, to whom the brothers now looked, shook her head. Never before, she said, had she occasion to trouble her brain about a light. When she wanted one in England, all she had to do was to call for one, or strike a match. What was to be done in their present circumstances she had not the smallest conception.

"I'll tell you what," said Otto, after several suggestions had been made and rejected, "this is how we'll do it. We will gather a lot of dry grass and dead sticks and build them up into a pile with logs around it, then Pina will sit down and gaze steadily at the heart of the pile for some minutes with her great, brown, sparkling eyes she should be able to kindle a flame in the heart of almost anything in five minutes—or, say ten, at the outside, eh?"

"I should think," retorted the Queen, "that your fiery spirit or flashing wit might accomplish the feat in a shorter time."

"It seems to me," remarked Dominick, who had been thinking too hard to pay much regard to these pleasantries, "that if we live long here we shall have to begin life over again—not our own lives, exactly, but the world's life. We shall have to invent everything anew for ourselves; discover new methods of performing old familiar work, and, generally, exercise our ingenuity to the uttermost."

"That may be quite true, you philosophic Premier," returned Otto, "but it does not light our fire, or roast that old hen which you brought down with a stone so cleverly to-day. Come, now, let us exercise our ingenuity a little more to the purpose, if possible."

"If we had only some tinder," said Dominick, "we could find flint, I dare say, or some hard kind of stone from which fire could be struck with the back of a clasp-knife, but I have seen nothing like tinder to-day. I've heard that burnt rag makes capital tinder. If so, a bit of Pina's dress might do, but we can't burn it without fire."

For a considerable time the trio sought to devise some means of procuring fire, but without success, and they were at last fain to content themselves with another cold supper of cocoa-nut and water, after which, being rather tired, they went to rest as on the previous night.

CHAPTER FOUR

DIFFICULTIES MET AND OVERCOME

The next day Pauline and her brothers visited the wreck, and here new difficulties met them, for although the vessel lay hard and fast on the rocks, there was a belt of water between it and the main shore, which was not only broad, but deep.

"I can easily swim it," said Dominick, beginning to pull off his coat.

"Dom," said Otto, solemnly, "sharks!"

"That's true, my boy, I won't risk it."

He put his coat on again, and turned to look for some drift-wood with which to make a raft.

"There's sure to be some lying about, you know," he said, "for a wreck could hardly take place without something or other in the way of spars or wreckage being washed ashore."

"But don't you think," suggested Otto, "that the men whose graves we have found may have used it all up?"

Otto was right. Not a scrap of timber or cordage of any kind was to be found after a most diligent search, and they were about to give it up in despair, when Pauline remembered the bay where they had been cast ashore, and which we have described as being filled with wreckage.

In truth, this bay and the reef with its group of islands lay right in the track of one of those great ocean currents which, as the reader probably knows, are caused by the constant circulation of all the waters of the sea between the equator and the poles. This grand and continuous flow is caused by difference of temperature and density in sea-water at different places. At the equator the water is warm, at the poles it is cold. This alone would suffice to cause circulation—somewhat as water circulates in a boiling pot—but other active agents are at work. The Arctic and Antarctic snows freshen the sea-water as well as cool it, while equatorial heat evaporates as well as warms it, and thus leaves a superabundance of salt and lime behind. The grand ocean current thus caused is broken up into smaller streams, and the courses of these are fixed by the conformation of land—just as a river's flow is turned right or left, and sometimes backward in eddies, by the form of its banks and bottom. Trade winds, and the earth's motion on its axis, still further modify the streams, both as to direction and force.

It was one of those currents, then, which flowed past the reef and sometimes cast vessels and wreckage on its shores.

Hastening to the bay, they accordingly found enough of broken spars and planks, to have made half a dozen rafts, twice the size of that required to go off with to the wreck; so to work they went at once with eager enthusiasm.

"Hold on!" shouted Dominick, after a few spars had been collected and dragged up on the sand.

Otto and Pauline paused in their labour, and looked anxiously at their brother, for his face wore a perplexed look.

"We have forgotten that it is impossible to shove a raft of any size, big or little, through these huge breakers, so as to get it round the point, to where the wreck lies."

"Well, then," cried Otto, with the ready assurance of ignorance, "we'll just drag it overland to the wreck, and launch it there."

"But, Otto, you have not taken into consideration the fact that our raft must be so large that, when finished, the dragging of it over rough ground would require three or four horses instead of three human beings."

"Well, then," returned the boy, "we'll make it small, just big enough to carry one person, and then we'll be able to drag it overland, and can go off to the wreck one at a time."

"Now, just think, brainless one," retorted Dominick; "suppose that I were to go off first to the wreck, what then?"

"Why, then *I* would go off next of course, and then Pina would follow, and so we'd all get on board one at a time, and explore it together."

"Yes; but what would you come off on?"

"The raft, to be sure."

"But the raft, I have supposed, is with me at the wreck. It won't go back to the shore of its own accord to fetch you, and we have no ropes with which to haul it to and fro."

"Then there's nothing for it," said Otto, after a few moments' thought, "but to make it big enough for two, or carry over the broken spars and planks piecemeal, and put them together opposite the wreck; so, come along."

This latter plan being adopted, they set to work with energy. To their joy they found not only that a good deal of cordage—somewhat worn, indeed, but still serviceable—was mingled with the wreckage, but that many large protruding bolts and rusty nails formed convenient holdfasts, which facilitated the building up and fastening together of the parts.

At last, after considerable labour, the raft was got ready early in the afternoon, and the brothers, embarking on it with two long poles, pushed off to the wreck while Pauline sat on the shore and watched them.

It was an anxious moment when they drew near enough to observe the vessel more distinctly, for it was just possible that they might find in her hold a supply of food and things they stood so much in need of, while, on the other hand, there was a strong probability that everything had been washed out of her long ago, or that her former crew had taken out all that was worth removing.

"What if we should find casks of biscuits and barrels of pork, to say nothing of tea and sugar, and such like?" murmured the sanguine Otto, as they poled slowly out.

"And what if we should find nothing at all?" said Dominick.

"O Dom!" exclaimed Otto, in a voice so despairing that his companion turned to look at him in surprise. "Look! see! the ship has been on fire! It can only be the mere skeleton that is left."

Dominick turned quickly, and saw that his brother had

reason for this remark. They had by that time approached so near to the wreck that the charred condition of part of her bulwarks, and specially of her lower spars, became obvious; and when, a few minutes later, they stood on the deck, the scene that presented itself was one of black desolation. Evidently the ill-fated vessel had been enveloped in flames, for everything on board was charred, and it was almost certain that her crew had run her on the rocks as the only method of escaping, her boats having been totally destroyed, as was apparent from the small portions of them that still hung from the davits.

"Nothing left!" said Otto. "I think that Robinson Crusoe himself would have given way to despair if *his* wreck had been anything like this. I wonder that even this much of it has been left above water after fire had got hold of it."

"Perhaps the hull sank after the first crash on the rocks, and put out the fire," suggested Dominick, "and then subsequent gales may have driven her higher up. Even now her stern lies pretty deep, and everything in her hold has been washed away."

There could be no doubt as to the latter point, for the deck had been blown up, probably by gunpowder, near the main-hatch, leaving a great hole, through which the hold could be seen almost as far as the bulkhead of the forecastle.

Hastening forward to the hatchway of this part of the vessel, in the feeble hope that they might still find something that would be of use, they descended quickly, but the first glance round quenched such a hope, for the fire had done its work there effectually, and, besides, there were obvious indications that, what the fire had spared, her crew had carried away. The only things left of any value were the charred remnants of the hammocks and bedding which had belonged to the sailors.

"Hurrah!" shouted Otto, with a sudden burst of joy, as he leaped forward and dragged out a quantity of the bedding; "here's what'll make fire at last! You said, Dom, that burnt rag was capital tinder. Well, here we have burnt sheets enough to last us for years to come!"

"That's true," returned Dominick, laughing at his brother's enthusiasm; "let's go aft and see if we can stumble on something more."

But the examination of the after part of the vessel yielded no fruit. As we have said, that part was sunk deeply, so that only the cabin skylight was above water, and, although they both gazed intently down through the water with which the cabin was filled, they could see nothing whatever. With a boat-hook which they found jammed in the port bulwarks, they poked and groped about for a considerable time, but hooked nothing, and were finally obliged to return empty-handed to the anxious Pauline.

Otto did not neglect, however, to carry off a pocketful of burnt-sheeting, by means of which, with flint and steel, they were enabled that night to eat their supper by the blaze of a cheering fire. The human heart when young, does not quickly or easily give way to despondency. Although the Rigondas had thus been cast on an island in the equatorial seas, and continued week after week to dwell there, living on wild fruits and eggs, and such animals and birds as they managed to snare, with no better shelter than a rocky cavern, and with little prospect of a speedy release, they did not by any means mourn over their lot.

"You see," remarked Otto, one evening when his sister wondered, with a sigh, whether their mother had yet begun to feel very anxious about them, "you see, she could not have expected to hear much before this time, for the voyage to Eastern seas is always a long one, and it is well known that vessels often get blown far out of their courses by monsoons, and simoons, and baboons, and such like southern hurricanes, so motherkins won't begin to grow anxious, I hope, for a long time yet, and it's likely that before she becomes *very* uneasy about us, some ship or other will pass close enough to see our signals and take us off so—"

"By the way," interrupted Dominick, "have you tried to climb our signal-tree, as you said you would do, to replace the flag that was blown away by last night's gale?"

"Of course not. There's no hurry, Dom," answered Otto, who, if truth must be told, was not very anxious to escape too soon from his present romantic position, and thought that it would be time enough to attract the attention of any passing vessel when they grew tired of their solitude. "Besides," he continued, with that tendency to self-defence which is so natural to fallen humanity, "I'm not a squirrel to run up the straight stem of a branchless tree, fifty feet high or more."

"No, my boy, you're not a squirrel, but, as I have often told you, you are a monkey—at least, monkey enough to accomplish your ends when you have a mind to."

"Now, really you are too hard," returned Otto, who was busily employed as he spoke in boring a hole through a cocoa-nut to get at the milk, "you know very well that the branch of the neighbouring tree by which we managed to reach the branches of the signal-tree has been blown away, so that the thing is impossible, for the stem is far too big to be climbed in the same way as I get up the cocoa-nut trees."

"That has nothing to do with the question," retorted Dominick, "you *said* you would try."

Otto looked with an injured expression at his sister and asked what she thought of a man being required to attempt impossibilities.

"Not a man—a monkey," interjected his brother.

"Whether man or monkey," said Pauline, in her quiet but decided way, "if you promised to attempt the thing, you are bound to try."

"Well, then, I will try, and here, I drink success to the trial." Otto applied the cocoa-nut to his lips, and took a long pull. "Come along, now, the sooner I prove the impossibility the better."

Rising at once, with an injured expression, the boy led the way towards a little eminence close at hand, on the top of which grew a few trees of various kinds, the tallest of these being the signal-tree, to which Dominick had fixed one of the half-burnt pieces of sheeting, brought from the wreck. The stem was perfectly straight and seemingly smooth, and as they stood at its foot gazing up to the fluttering little piece of rag that still adhered to it, the impossibility of the ascent became indeed very obvious.

"Now, sir, are you convinced?" said Otto.

"No, sir, I am not convinced," returned Dominick.

"You said you would try."

Without another word Otto grasped the stem of the tree with arms and legs, and did his best to ascend it. He had, in truth, so much of the monkey in him, and was so wiry and tough, that he succeeded in getting up full twelve or fourteen feet before being utterly exhausted. At that point, however, he stuck, but instead of slipping down as he had intended, and again requesting to know whether his brother was convinced, he uttered a sharp cry, and shouted—

"Oh! I say, Dom, what am I to do?"

"Why, slip down, of course."

"But I can't. The bark seems to be made of needle-joints, all sticking upwards. If I try to slip, my trousers vill remain behind, and—and—I can't hold on much longer!"

"Let go then, and drop," said Dominick, stepping close to the tree.

"Oh no, don't!" cried Pauline, with a little shriek; "if you do you'll—you'll—"

"Bust! Yes, I know I shall," shouted Otto, in despair.

"No fear," cried Dominick, holding out his arms, "let go, I'll cat—"

He was stopped abruptly by receiving a shock from his little brother which sent him sprawling on his back. He sprang up, however, with a gasp.

"Why, boy, I had no idea you were so heavy," he exclaimed, laughing.

"Now, don't you go boasting in future, you prime minister, that I can't knock you down," said Otto, as he gathered himself up. "But I say, you're not hurt, are you?" he added, with a look of concern, while Pauline seized one of Dominick's hands and echoed the question.

"Not in the least—only a little wind knocked out of me. Moreover, I'm not yet convinced that the ascent of that tree is an impossibility."

"You'll have to do it yourself, then," said Otto; "and let me warn you beforehand that, though I'm very grateful to you, I won't stand under to catch you."

"Was it not you who said the other night at supper that whatever a fellow resolved to do he could accomplish, and added that, where there's a will, there's a way?"

"I rather think it was you, Dom, who gave expression to those boastful sentiments."

"It may be so. At all events I hold them. Come, now, lend a hand and help me. The work will take some time, as we have no other implements than our gully-knives, but we'll manage it somehow."

"Can I not help you?" asked Pauline.

"Of course you can. Sit down on the bank here, and I'll give you something to do presently."

Dominick went, as he spoke, to a small tree, the bark of which was long, tough, and stringy. Cutting off a quantity of this, he took it to his sister, and showed her how to twist some of it into stout cordage. Leaving her busily at work on this, he went down to the nearest bamboo thicket and cut a stout cane. It took some time to cut, for the bamboo was hard and the knife small for such work. From the end of the cane he cut off a piece about a foot in length.

"Now, Otto, my boy, you split that into four pieces, and sharpen the end of each piece, while I cut off another foot of the bamboo."

"But what are you going to do with these bits of stick?" asked Otto, as he went to work with a will.

"You shall see. No use in wasting time with explanations just now. I read of the plan in a book of travels. There's nothing like a good book of travels to put one up to numerous dodges."

"I'm not so sure o' that," objected the boy. "I have read *Robinson Crusoe* over and over, and over again, and I don't recollect reading of his having made use of pegs to climb trees with."

"Your memory may be at fault, perhaps. Besides, Robinson's is not the only book of travels in the world," returned Dominick, as he hacked away at the stout bamboo.

"No; but it is certainly the best," returned Otto, with enthusiasm, "and I mean to imitate its hero."

"Don't do that, my boy," said Dominick; "whatever you do, don't imitate. Act well the part allotted to you, whatever it may be, according to the promptings of your own particular nature; but don't imitate."

"Humph! I won't be guided by your wise notions, Mr Premier. All I know is, that I wish my clothes would wear out faster, so that I might dress myself in skins of some sort. I would have made an umbrella by this time, but it never seems to rain in this country."

"Ha! Wait till the rainy season comes round, and you'll have more than enough of it. Come, we've got enough of pegs to begin with. Go into the thicket now; cut some of the longest bamboos you can find, and bring them to me; six or eight will do—slender ones, about twice the thickness of my thumb at the ground."

While Otto was engaged in obeying this order, his brother returned to the signal-tree.

"Well done, Pina," he said; "you've made some capital cordage."

"What are you going to do now, brother?"

"You shall see," said Dominick, picking up a heavy stone to use as a hammer, with which he drove one of the hard, sharp pegs into the tree, at about three feet from the ground. We have said the peg was a foot long. As he fixed it in the tree about three inches deep, nine inches of it projected. On this he placed his foot and raised himself to test its strength. It bore his weight well. Above this first peg he fixed a second, three feet or so higher, and then a third about level with his face.

"Ah! I see," exclaimed Otto, coming up at that moment with several long bamboos. "But, man, don't you see that if one of these pegs should give way while you're driving those above it, down you come by the run, and, if you should be high up at the time, death will be probable—lameness for life, certain."

Dominick did not condescend to answer this remark, but, taking one of the bamboos, stood it up close to the tree, not touching, but a few inches from the trunk, and bound it firmly with the cord to the three pegs. Thus he had the first three rounds or rungs of an upright ladder, one side of which was the tree, the other the bamboo. Mounting the second of these rungs he drove in a fourth peg, and fastened the bamboo to it in the same way, and then, taking another step, he fixed a fifth peg. Thus, step by step, he mounted till he had reached between fifteen and twenty feet from the ground, where the upright bamboo becoming too slender, another was called for and handed up by Otto. This was lashed to the first bamboo, as well as to three of the highest pegs, and the operation was continued. When the thin part of the second long bamboo was reached, a third was added; and so the work progressed until the ladder was completed, and the lower branches of the tree were gained.

Long before that point, however, Otto begged to be allowed to continue and finish the work, which his brother agreed to, and, finally, the signal flag was renewed, by the greater part of an old hammock being lashed to the top of the tree.

But weeks and months passed away, and the flag continued to fly without attracting the attention of any one more important, or more powerful to deliver them, than the albatross and the wild sea-mew.

During this period the ingenuity and inventive powers of the party were taxed severely, for, being utterly destitute of tools of any kind, with the exception of the gully-knives before mentioned, they found it extremely difficult to fashion any sort of implement.

"If we had only an axe or a saw," said Otto one morning, with a groan of despair, "what a difference it would make."

"Isn't there a proverb," said Pauline, who at the time was busy making cordage while Otto was breaking sticks for the fire, "which says that we never know our mercies till we lose them?"

R. M. Ballantyne

"Perhaps there is," said Otto, "and if there isn't, I don't care. I don't like proverbs, they always tell you in an owlishly wise sort o' way what you know only too well, at a time when you'd rather not know it if possible. Now, if we only had an axe—ever so small—I would be able to fell trees and cut 'em up into big logs, instead of spending hours every day searching for dead branches and breaking them across my knee. It's not a pleasant branch of our business, I can tell you."

"But you have the variety of hunting," said his sister, "and that, you know, is an agreeable as well as useful branch."

"Humph! It's not so agreeable as I used to think it would be, when one has to run after creatures that run faster than one's-self, and one is obliged to use wooden spears, and slings, instead of guns. By the way, what a surprising, I may say awful, effect a well-slung stone has on the side of a little pig! I came upon a herd yesterday in the cane-brake, and, before they could get away, I slung a big stone at them, which caught the smallest of the squeakers fair in the side. The sudden squeal that followed the slap was so intense, that I thought the life had gone out of the creature in one agonising gush; but it hadn't, so I slung another stone, which took it in the head and dropt it."

"Poor thing! I wonder how you can be so cruel."

"Cruel!" exclaimed Otto, "I don't do it for pleasure, do I? Pigs and other things have got to be killed if we are to live."

"Well, I suppose so," returned Pauline, with a sigh; "at all events it would never do to roast and eat them alive. But, about the axe. Is there no iron-work in the wreck that might be fashioned into one?"

"Oh yes, sister dear," returned Otto, with a short laugh, "there's plenty of iron-work. Some crowbars and ringbolts, and an anchor or two; but do you suppose that I can slice off a bit of an anchor in the shape of an axe as you slice a loaf?"

"Well no, not exactly, but I thought there might be some small flat pieces that could be made to do."

"What is your difficulty," asked Dominick, returning from a hunting expedition at that moment, and flinging down three brace of fowls on the floor of the golden cave.

When the difficulty was stated, he remarked that he had often pondered the matter while lying awake at night, and when wandering in the woods; and he had come to the conclusion that they must return to what was termed the stone period of history, and make their axes of flint.

Otto shook his head, and thought Pina's idea of searching the wreck till they found a piece of flat metal was a more hopeful scheme.

"What do you say to trying both plans?" cried Pauline, with sudden animation. "Come, as you have voluntarily elected me queen of this realm, I command you, Sir Dominick, to make a flint axe without delay, and you, Sir Otto, to make an iron one without loss of time."

"Your majesty shall be obeyed," replied her obedient subjects, and to work they went accordingly, the very next morning.

Dominick searched far and near for a flint large enough for his purpose. He found several, and tried to split them by laying them on a flat stone, upheaving another stone as large as he could lift, and hurling it down on them with all his might. Sometimes the flint would fly from under the stone without being broken, sometimes it would be crushed to fragments, and at other times would split in a manner that rendered it quite unsuitable. At last, however, by patient perseverance, he succeeded in splitting one so that an edge of it was thin and sharp, while the other end was thick and blunt.

Delighted with this success, he immediately cut with his knife, a branch of one of the hardest trees he could find, and formed it into an axe-handle. Some of Pauline's cord he tied round the middle of this, and then split it at one end, using his flint for the purpose, and a stone for a hammer. The split extended only as far as the cord, and he forced it open by means of little stones as wedges until it was wide enough to admit the thick end of his flint axe-head. Using a piece of soft stone as a pencil, he now marked the form of the flint, where it touched the wood, exactly, and worked at this with his knife, as patiently as a Chinaman, for several hours, until the wood fitted the irregularities and indentations of the flint to a nicety. This of itself caused the wood to hold the flint-head very firmly. Then the wedges were removed, and when the handle was bound all round the split part with cord, and the flint-head enveloped in the same, the whole thing became like a solid mass.

Gingerly and anxiously did Dominick apply it to a tree. To his joy his axe caused the chips to fly in all directions. He soon stopped, however, for fear of breaking it, and set off in triumph to the golden cave.

Meanwhile Otto, launching the raft, went on board the wreck to search for a suitable bit of iron. As he had said, there was plenty on board, but none of the size or shape that he required, and he was about to quit in despair when he observed the flat iron plates, about five inches square and quarter of an inch thick, with a large hole in the centre of each, which formed the sockets that held the davits for suspending the ship's boats. A crowbar enabled him, after much trouble, to wrench off one of these. A handspike was, after some hours' labour, converted into a handle with one side cut flat. Laying the plate on this, he marked its exact size, and then cut away the wood until the iron sank its own thickness into it. There were plenty of nails in the wreck; with these he nailed the iron, through its own nail-holes, to the hard handspike, and, still further to secure it, he covered it with a little piece of flat wood, which he bound firmly on with some cordage made by his sister from cocoa-nut fibre. As the iron projected on both sides of the handle, it thus formed a double-edged axe of the most formidable appearance. Of course the edges required grinding down, but this was a mere matter of detail, to be accomplished by prolonged and patient rubbing on a stone!

Otto arrived triumphantly at the golden cave almost at the same moment with his brother, and they both laid their axes at the feet of the queen.

"Thanks, my trusty vassals," she said; "I knew you would both succeed, and had prepared a royal feast against your return."

"To which I have brought a royal appetite, your majesty," said Otto.

"In truth so have I," added Dominick.

There was a good deal of jesting in all this; nevertheless the trio sat down to supper that night highly pleased with themselves. While eating, they discussed, with much animation, the merits of the axes, and experienced no little difficulty in deciding which was the better tool. At last

R. M. Ballantyne

Pauline settled the matter by declaring that the iron axe, being the strongest, was, perhaps, the best; but as it was not yet sharpened, while Dominick's was ready for immediate use, the flint axe was in present circumstances better.

"So then, being equal," said Otto, "and having had a splendid supper, we will retire to rest."

Thus, in devising means for increasing their comforts, and supplying their daily necessities, the days and weeks flew swiftly by.

CHAPTER FIVE

STIRRING EVENTS AND CHANGES

An event was now pending over the castaway family which was destined to darken their bright sky, and interrupt them in the even tenor of their way.

Up to this time the interest, not to say delight, with which they went about their daily avocations, the fineness of the weather, and the romance of their situation, had prevented their minds from dwelling much on the flight of time, and if Pauline had not remembered the Sundays by conscientiously keeping a daily record with a pencil on a piece of bark, not one of them would have believed it possible that two months had elapsed since they were cast ashore.

The sanguine hope, too, which filled the breast of each, that a vessel would certainly pass by sooner or later and take them off, prevented their being disturbed by gloomy anticipations of a long exile, and it is probable that they would have gone on pleasantly for a much longer time, improving the golden cave, and exploring the reef, and developing the resources of what Otto styled the Queendom, without much caring about the future, had not the event above referred to come upon them with the sudden violence of a thunder-clap, terminating their peaceful life in a way they had never anticipated, and leading to changes which the wildest imagination could hardly have conceived.

That event was, indeed, the arrival of a ship, but it did not arrive in the manner that had been expected. It came in the dead of a dark night, when the elements seemed to have declared fierce war against each other, for it was difficult to say whether the roaring of the sea, the crashing of the thunder, or the flashing of the forked lightning was most tremendous.

A previous storm or two, of a mild type, having warned our trio that Paradise had not been quite regained, even in that lovely region, they had fitted something like a front, formed of wreckage, to the golden cave, and this had, up to that time, formed a sufficient protection against slight inclemencies of weather; but on this particular night the gusts of wind were so violent, and shook the front of their dwelling so much, that both Dominick and his brother found it impossible to sleep. Their sister, however, lay undisturbed, because she reposed in an inner chamber, which had been screened off with broken planks, and these not only checked draughts, but deadened sounds.

"I'm afraid our wall will come down," said Dominick, raising himself at last on one elbow, and gazing at the wooden erection uneasily.

"Oh, let it come!" growled Otto, who had been so frequently checked while dropping into slumber that night that he was getting quite cross.

Not feeling quite so regardless of consequences, his brother Dominick arose and endeavoured to prop the weak part of the structure with an additional piece of timber.

He had accomplished his object, and was about to lie down again to rest, when a terrible cry was heard, which rose above the roaring of the storm. There seemed something so appalling in it, and at the same time so unaccountable in that solitary spot, that Dominick's heart almost stood still for a moment with superstitious fear. Otto also heard the cry, and sat bolt upright, while drowsiness was effectually banished from his brain.

"Dom, did you hear that?" he asked in a solemn voice. "I should think I did," replied his brother in a low tone. The cave being very dark, neither could see the other distinctly. They sat silent for a few moments, anxiously listening for a repetition of the cry.

"Move quietly, Otto," said Dominick, as he crept towards their little door, "it evidently has not awaked Pina, and we may as well let her lie still till we find out what it is."

"You're not going out, Dom?" asked Otto, in anxiety.

"Yes, why not?"

"Be—because—it—it may be—be—something—*awful*!"

"It *must* be something awful, and that is just why I am going out. Come, you didn't use to be a coward."

This was touching the boy on a tender point. He was indeed by no means a coward when the danger he had to face was comprehensible and obvious, but when the danger happened to be incomprehensible, as well as invisible, his courage was not quite as high as might have been desired. The taunt of his brother stirred up his pride however. He rose and followed him in silence, with stern resolve and a quaking heart!

On issuing from their shelter the brothers had to lean heavily against the blast to prevent their being swept away. Seeking the shelter of a bush, they gazed around them, but saw nothing save a dim appearance of bending trees and scudding foam.

"The cry may have come from the beach; let's go down," said Dominick, leaving the shelter of the bush, and pushing forward.

"Better go back," was on Otto's lips, but he repressed the words and followed.

There was not light enough to enable them to see objects on land, but whatever chanced to be pictured against the dark sky became distinctly visible as a dark object. The old familiar wreck was therefore seen the moment they cleared the bushes that fringed the bay, but close to it was another object which was very unfamiliar indeed to their eyes. It accounted for the cry and caused a gush of mingled feelings in the breasts of the brothers.

Let us now, good reader, wing our flight out to sea, and backwards a little in time. On that stormy night of which we treat, a large emigrant ship was scudding before the gale almost under bare poles. Part of her sails and rigging had been carried away; the rest of her was more or less damaged. The officers, having had no reliable observation for several days, were not sure of their exact position on the great ocean, and the captain, being well aware of the danger of those seas, was filled with anxiety. To add to his troubles, the crew had become slightly mutinous, and some of the emigrants—of whom there were upwards of three hundred on board—sided with the crew. It was even whispered that the chief mate was at the bottom of a plot to murder the captain and seize the ship. For what purpose, of course, no one could tell, and, indeed, there was no apparent ground for the rumour, beyond the fact that the mate—Malines by name—was a surly, taciturn man, with a scowling, though handsome, visage, and a powerful frame.

But whatever of truth might have been in these rumours was never brought to light, for an accident occurred during the gale which put the commander of the vessel beyond the power of earthly foes. One of the larger ropes of the vessel snapt, and the heavy block attached to it swung against the captain with such violence as to kill him on the spot. The momentary confusion which followed the disaster distracted the attention of the steersman, and a heavy sea was shipped, by which the captain's body was swept overboard. No attempt was made to lower a boat or check the ship. Even the unskilled emigrants understood that no boat could live in such a sea, and that rescue was impossible. The vessel held on her wild course as if nothing had happened.

Malines, being now in command, issued an order that all the emigrants should go below, and the hatches be secured.

The women and children and most of the men were already in their uncomfortable quarters below hatches, but a group of hardy-looking fellows, who held on to ropes and stanchions near the windlass, refused to move. Among them was a remarkably powerful woman, whose tongue afforded presumptive evidence that she had been born in the Emerald Isle.

"We'll stop where we be, master," said one of the emigrants, with a quiet but resolute air.

"That's right, Joe, stick up. We ain't slaves," said another.

To this last speaker Malines turned fiercely and knocked him down; then, seizing him by the collar and dragging him to the hatchway, he thrust him below. It may be remarked that the man thus roughly treated—Redding by name—was a little man. Bullies usually select little men when inclined to display their courage.

"Shame on yez," exclaimed the Irish woman, clenching her huge fist. "If it wasn't that I'm a poor widdy woman, I'd—I'd—"

"Howld yer tongue, Mother Lynch," whispered a lively youth of about nineteen by her side, who obviously hailed from the same country. "It's not aggravatin' him that'll do *him* good. Let him be, darlin', and he'll soon blow the steam off."

"An' what does it matter to me, Teddy Malone, whether he blows the steam off, or keeps it down till he bursts his biler? Is it a descendant o' the royal family o' Munster as'll howld her tongue whin she sees cruelty and injustice?"

Without paying the slightest regard to this royal personage, Malines returned to the group of men, and repeated his order to go below; but they did not go, and he seized a handspike with a view to enforce his commands. He hesitated, however, on observing that the man named Joe, after quietly buttoning his coat, was turning up his wristbands as if in preparation for a pugilistic encounter.

"Lookee here now, Mister Malines," said Joe, with a mild, even kindly, expression, which was the very reverse of belligerent; "I was allers a law-abidin' man myself, and don't have no love for fightin'; but when I'm ordered to go into a dark hole, and have the lid shut down on me an' locked, I feels a sort of objection, d'ee see. If you lets us be, us'll let you be. If otherwise—"

Joe stopped abruptly, grinned, and clenched his enormous fists.

Mr Malines was one of those wise men who know when they have met their match. His knockings down and overbearing ways always stopped short at that line where he met courage and strength equal or superior to his own. He possessed about the average of bull-dog courage and more than the average of physical strength, but observing that Joe was gifted with still more of both these qualities, he lowered the handspike, and with a sneer replied—

"Oh, well—please yourselves. It matters nothing to me if you get washed overboard. Make all fast, lads," he added, turning to his crew, who stood prepared for what one of them styled a scrimmage. Malines returned to the quarter-deck, followed by a half-suppressed laugh from some of the mutinous emigrants.

"You see, David," remarked Joe, in a quiet tone, to a man beside him, as he turned down his cuffs, "I think, from the look of him, that if we was to strike on rocks, or run on shore, or take to sinking, or anything o' that sort, the mate is mean enough to look arter hisself and leave the poor things below to be choked in a hole. So you an' me must keep on deck, so as to let 'em all out if need be."

"Right, Joe, right you are."

The man who thus replied bore such a strong resemblance to Joe in grave kindliness of expression and colossal size of frame, that even a stranger could not fail to recognise them as brothers, and such they were—in truth they were twins, having first seen the light together just thirty years before. There was this difference in the character of the brothers, however, that Joe Binney was the more intellectual and resolute of the two. David Binney, recognising this fact, and loving his brother with all the fervour of a strong nature, was in the habit of looking up to him for advice, and submitting to him as if he had been an elder brother. Nevertheless, David was not without a mind of his own, and sometimes differed in opinion with Joe. He even occasionally disputed, but never with the slightest tinge of ill-feeling.

While the brothers were conversing in an undertone on the dangers of the sea, and the disagreeables of a fore-cabin, the mass of unfortunates below were cowering in their berths, rendered almost forgetful of the stifling atmosphere, and the wailing of sick children, by the fear of shipwreck, as they listened with throbbing hearts to the howling wind and rattling cordage overhead, and felt the tremendous shocks when the good ship was buffeted by the sea.

Near to Joe Binney stood one of the sailors on outlook. He was a dark-complexioned, savage-looking man, who had done more than any one else to foment the bad feeling that had existed between the captain and his men.

"Ye look somethin' skeared, Hugh Morris," said Joe, observing that the look-out was gazing over the bow with an expression of alarm.

"Breakers ahead!" roared the man at that moment—"port!— hard-a-port!"

The order was sharply repeated, and promptly obeyed, and the vessel came round in time to escape destruction on a ledge of rocks, over which the water was foaming furiously.

Instantly Malines went forward and began to give hurried directions to the steersman. The danger was avoided, though the escape was narrow, and the low rocks were seen passing astern, while the sea ahead seemed to be free from obstruction, as far, at least, as the profound darkness permitted them to see.

"They'll be all drowned like rats in a hole if we strike," muttered the sailor, Hugh Morris, as if speaking to himself.

"Not if I can help it," said Joe Binney, who overheard the remark.

As he spoke he went to the little companion hatch, or door to the fore-cabin, and tried to open it, but could not.

"Here, David," he cried, "lend a hand."

Applying their united strength—with some assistance from Teddy Malone, and earnest encouragement from Mrs Lynch—they succeeded in bursting open the hatch.

"Hallo! there," shouted Joe, in a voice that would have been creditable to a boatswain, "come on deck if ye don't want to be drownded."

"Hooroo!" added Malone, "we're goin' to the bottom! Look alive wid ye."

"Ay, an' bring up the childers," yelled Mrs Lynch. "Don't lave wan o' thim below."

Of course, the poor emigrants were not slow to obey these startling orders.

The state of affairs was so serious that Malines either did not see, or did not care for, what was going on. He stood on the forecastle looking out intently ahead.

"Land on the starboard beam!" shouted Morris suddenly.

The mate was on the point of giving an order to the steersman when he observed land looming on the port bow. Instantly he saw that all hope was over. They were steering to inevitable destruction between two ledges of rock! What he would have done in the circumstances no one can tell, because before he had time to act the vessel struck with great violence, and the terror-stricken passengers gave vent to that appalling cry of fear which had so suddenly aroused Dominick Rigonda and his brother.

As the vessel remained hard and fast, with her bow thrust high on the rocks, the emigrants and crew found a partial refuge from the violence of the waves on the forecastle. Hence the first wild shriek of fear was not repeated. In a few minutes, however, a wave of greater size than usual came rushing towards the vessel. Fortunately, most of the emigrants failed to realise the danger, but the seamen were fully alive to it.

"It's all over with us," exclaimed the mate, in a sort of reckless despair. But he was wrong. The great billow, which he expected would dash the vessel in pieces—and which, in nine cases out of ten, would have done so—lifted the wreck so high as to carry it almost completely over the ledge, on which it had struck, leaving the stern high on the rocks, while the bow was plunged into the partly-protected water on the other side.

The sudden descent of the forecastle induced the belief an many of the emigrants' minds that they were about to go headlong to the bottom, and another cry of terror arose; but when they found that their place of refuge sank no further than to a level with the water, most of them took heart again, and began to scramble up to the quarter-deck as hastily as they had before scrambled to the forecastle.

"Something like land ahead," observed Hugh Morris, who stood close to the mate.

"I don't see it," returned the latter, gruffly, for he was jealous of the influence that Morris had over the crew, and, during the whole voyage, had treated him harshly.

"It may be there, although you don't see it," retorted Hugh, with a feeling of scorn, which he made no attempt to conceal.

"Sure I sees somethin' movin' on the wather," exclaimed Mrs Lynch, who, during the occurrences just described, had held on to a belaying pin with the tenacity and strength of an octopus.

"It's the wather movin' in yer own eyes, mother," said Malone, who stood beside his Amazonian countrywoman.

At that moment a halloo was heard faintly in the distance, and, soon after, a raft was seen approaching, guided, apparently, by two men.

"Raft a-hoy! Where d'ee hail from?" shouted the mate.

"From nowhere!" came back promptly in a boy's ringing voice.

"You've got on a coral reef," shouted a powerful voice, which, we need scarcely say, was that of Dominick Rigonda, "but you're safe enough now. The last wave has shoved you over into sheltered water. You're in luck. We'll soon put you on shore."

R. M. Ballantyne

"An island, I suppose," said Malines, as the raft came alongside. "What may be its name?"

"Got no name that I know of; as far as I know it's uninhabited, and, probably, unknown. Only three of us here—wrecked like yourselves. If you have boats, lower them, and I'll pilot you to land."

"Ohone!" groaned Mrs Lynch, in solemn despair, as she tried to see the speaker, whom darkness rendered almost invisible. "An unbeknown island, uninhabited by nobody. Boys, we are done for intirely. Didn't I say this would be the end of it, when we made up our minds to go to say?"

No one seemed inclined just then to dispute the prophetic reminiscences of the widow, for the order had been given to get ready one of the boats. Turning to the emigrants, who were now clustering on the fore part of the vessel, Malines, condescending to adopt a more respectful tone, addressed them as follows:—

"Now, let me tell you, one and all, that your voyage has come to an end sooner than I expected. Our ship is wrecked, but we're out of danger, and must go ashore an' live as best we can, or die if we can't live. Where we are, I don't know, and don't care, for it don't much matter. It's an island, it seems, and three people who have been wrecked before us are all its population. As it is too dark to go ashore comfortably to-night, I would advise you to go below again, an' turn in till daylight. You may make your minds easy, for there's no fear of our going to the bottom *now*."

"Sure, an' you're right there," murmured Teddy Malone, "for aren't we at the bottom already?"

"You may all do as you please, however," continued the

mate, after a low-toned remark from one of the crew, "for my command has come to an end with the loss of the ship."

When the mate ceased speaking, there was a brief pause, for the unfortunate emigrants had been so long accustomed to conform to the strict discipline of the ship that they felt like sheep suddenly deprived of a shepherd, or soldiers bereft of their officers when thus left to think for themselves. Then the self-sufficient and officious among them began to give advice, and to dispute noisily as to what they should do, so that in a few minutes their voices, mingling with the gale and the cries of terrified children, caused such a din that the strong spirit of the widow Lynch was stirred within her, inducing her to raise her masculine voice in a shout that silenced nearly all the rest.

"That's right, mother," cried young Malone, "howld yer tongues, boys, and let's hear what the widdy has to say. Isn't it herself has got the great mind—not to mintion the body?"

"Shut your murphy-trap, Teddy," retorted the widow, "an' here's what I've got to say. We must have only wan man to guide us if we are to get on at all. Too many cooks, ye knows well enough, is sure to spile the broth. Let Joe Binney speak, and the rest of 'ee howld yer tongues, if ye can."

Thus invited, modest Joe gave it as his opinion that the emigrants could not do better than follow the advice of Muster Malines—go below, turn in, and wait till daylight. He added further that he would count it a favour if Muster Malines would continue in command of the party, at least till they all got ashore.

This little compliment to the man whom he had so recently defied had a softening influence on the mate, and the proposal was well received by the people, who, even during

R. M. Ballantyne

the few minutes of anarchy which had prevailed, were led to appreciate the value of order and government.

"You are right, Binney," said the mate. "I would advise you all, good people, to go below and rest as well as you can, while I, and those who choose to act under me, will go ashore and make the best possible arrangements for your landing in the morning."

"Now, why don't ye do what ye'er towld at wanst?" cried Mrs Lynch, who had evidently made up her mind that the reins of government were not to be entirely given up to the mate. "It's not wishin', are ye, to get wetter than ye are, a'ready? Go below, ivery wan of ye."

Like a meek flock, the women and children obeyed the mandate, being absolutely in bodily fear of the woman, while most of the men followed them with a laugh, or a little chaff, according to temperament.

Before the latter had left the deck, Malines suggested that Joe Binney and his brother David should accompany him on shore that night, to represent the emigrants, as it were, and assist him in the proposed arrangements.

"Besides," he added, "there is just the possibility that we may fall into a trap. We know nothing about the man who has come off to us except his voice, so that it will be wise to land with some of our best men armed."

Of course the brothers had no objection to this plan, and accordingly they, with the mate and four of the ship's crew—all armed with cutlasses and pistols—got into one of the boats and were lowered into the water on the lee side of the vessel, where Dominick and Otto had been quietly awaiting the end of the foregoing discussions.

In a few minutes they reached the shore, and then Dominick shook hands with them, and welcomed them to the islands, "which," he said, "we have named 'Refuge Islands.'"

"Run up to the cave, Otto," he whispered, while the party was engaged in drawing up the boat. "Stir up the fire and rouse Pina,—tell her to prepare to receive company."

"She'll be as much puzzled as if I told her to prepare to receive cavalry," muttered the boy as he ran up to the cave.

"Hallo! Pina! rouse up, old girl," he shouted, bursting into the cave, and falling on his knees before the embers of the fire, which he soon blew up into a flame. "I say, Pina! hallo! Pina! Pi-i-i-i-na!"

"Dear me, Otto, what is wrong?" asked the sleepy voice of Pauline from behind her screen.

"Wrong?" cried her brother, "nothing's wrong—that is, everything's wrong; but don't be afraid, old girl, all's right. Dress as fast as you can, and prepare for company!"

"What *do* you mean?" cried the girl, by that time thoroughly aroused, and somewhat alarmed by Otto's words and excitement.

"Can't explain. No time. Get up, make yourself presentable, and come out of your den."

As he spoke Pauline lifted the curtain door of her apartment and stepped into the outer cave, which was by that time all aglow with the ruddy blaze.

"Do you call yourself presentable?" asked Otto, laughing; "why your hair is raised like the back of a wild cat."

It is only right to say that the boy did not do his sister justice. An old shawl thrown hastily on, and descending in confused folds around her slight, graceful figure, invested her with an air of classic simplicity, while her pretty face, surrounded by a wealth of dishevelled, but beautiful, hair, was suggestive of something very much the reverse of a wild cat.

"Are you prepared, sister, for a stunning surprise?" said Otto, quickly, for he heard the approaching footsteps of the party.

"I'm prepared for anything," said Pauline, her lustrous eyes and her little mouth opening simultaneously, for she also heard the numerous footfalls outside.

"'Tis well!" cried Otto, starting up, and assuming a heroic attitude as he waved his right hand toward the door of the cavern, "no time to explain. Enter Dominick, with band of robbers, headed by their captain, amid shrieking wind, forked lightning, and peals of thunder!"

As he spoke, Pauline, despite her surprise, could scarcely refrain from laughter, for Otto's words were fulfilled almost to the letter. Amid a strife of elements that caused their frail erections to tremble, the little door burst open, and Dominick, stooping low to save his head, entered. He was followed by the gaunt, dark form of Malines, who, in rough garments and long fishermen's boots, with pistols in belt, and cutlass by his side, was a particularly good representative of a robber-captain. Following him came the still more gigantic Joe Binney, and his equally huge brother David, after which trooped in the boat's crew one by one.

As each man entered he stood stock still—dumb, petrified with astonishment—as he gazed, saucer-eyed, at Pauline. Bereft of speech and motion, she returned the gaze with interest.

Oh! it was a rare treat to Otto! His little bosom heaved with delight as he watched the shipwrecked men enter one after another and become petrefactions! Some of the sailors even dropped their lower jaws with wonder.

Dominick, who, in the bustle of action, had not thought of the surprise in store for his visitors, burst into a hearty fit of laughter.

"It was well got up, Otto," he said at last.

"No, it wasn't, Dom. I do assure you it was not got up at all, but came about in the most natural manner."

"Well, got up or not," returned Dominick, "here you are, friends, in what we have styled our golden cave, and this is my sister Pauline—allow me to introduce you, Pina, to part of a shipwrecked crew."

The youth's laughter, and the introduction which followed, seemed to disenchant the mariners, who, recovering self-possession with a deep sigh, became sheepish in bearing, and seemed inclined to beat a retreat, but our heroine quickly put them at their ease. With a natural tact and grace of manner which had the appearance of, but was not meant for, dignity, she advanced and offered her little hand to Malines, who seemed to fear that he might crush it unintentionally, so slight was the shake he gave it.

"You are heartily welcome to our cavern," she said. "I'm *so* grieved to hear that you have been wrecked."

"Don't mention it, Miss. Not worth speaking of, I assure you; we're quite used to it," replied Malines, not knowing very well what he said.

The ice, however, was broken. From this point all went on, as Otto said, swimmingly. The mate began to relate the circumstances of the recent wreck, while Pauline and Otto spread the remains of their supper before the men, and set about roasting the fowls that had been intended for the morrow's breakfast.

Before long the gale began to abate, and the sailors went out with Dominick, to select a spot on which the emigrants might encamp, being aided in this work by a struggling and fitful moonlight. After that Malines went back with his party to the ship, and Dominick returned with Otto to court slumber in the golden cave.

CHAPTER SIX

SHIPWRECKED EMIGRANTS
AND HORRIFIED CONSPIRATORS

The scene which presented itself on the morning after the storm is not easily described, and the change to the trio who had up to that time lived so peacefully on Refuge Islands' Reef was so great that they found it difficult at first to believe it was other than a dream.

On awaking, indeed, Otto saluted his brother with the exclamation—

"O Dom, I've had such a comical dream!"

"Indeed, my boy," said Dominick, "I fear it was no dream, but a reality."

At this Otto suddenly sprang up, and ran out to relieve his mind on the point. A few seconds sufficed. On clearing the bushes he beheld the new wreck lying not far from the old one, and saw from the crowds of people who were being put into the boats that the emigrant ship had been no mere creature of his imagination. It was evident that the boat which had just quitted the vessel's side contained the first band of emigrants, for the only people yet landed were a few

R. M. Ballantyne

men, who busied themselves in putting up a rude shelter for the women and children, and in kindling fires for the preparation of breakfast on a little mound between two and three hundred yards from the golden cave.

By that time the storm had blown itself out, and the rising sun was mounting into a cloudless blue sky, and covering the sea with dazzling ripples, which looked as if the very water were laughing with joy at the sudden change from darkness and fury to light and peace.

Conspicuous among those who worked on shore was the gigantic form of Joe Binney. Considering him an old acquaintance. Otto ran up to him and shook hands.

"How many emigrants are there of you?" he asked.

"Three hundred, more or less, master, but I ain't rightly sure; there's such a many that it's difficult to count 'em when they are all a-movin' to and fro."

"Here, Joe, catch hold o' this post, an' keep it steady till I make it fast," said Hugh Morris, the seaman who has been described as one of the most turbulent among the men.

While Joe assisted in the erection of the canvas booth or shelter, he gave Otto a good deal of information regarding the vessel, the emigrants, the crew, and the misunderstandings which had occurred previous to the captain's death.

"It's well for one man that we've bin wrecked, anyhow," remarked Morris, stepping back with an artistic air to survey his handiwork.

"You mean the young doctor," said Joe.

"That's who I mean," returned Morris. "Doctor John Marsh. He's the only man in the ship that's worth his salt, but I fear he's a doomed man."

"I hope not, Hugh, though there *are* one or two men on board worth more than their salt," said Joe, with a peculiar smile, as he returned to the care of a large kettle of beans, from which the sailor had called him.

On Otto inquiring what was the matter with the doctor, Joe Binney explained—

"He's been ill a'most since we left England, owin' to a fall he had in tryin' to save one o' the child'n as was tumblin' down the after-hatch. He saved the child, but broke one or two of his own ribs, an' the broken ends must have damaged his lungs, for, ever since, he's bin spittin' blood an' wearin' away, till we can hardly believe he's the same stout, hearty, active young feller that came aboord at Gravesend. Spite of his hurt he's bin goin' among us quite cheerful-like, doin' the best he could for the sick; but as Morris says, he looks like a doomed man. P'r'aps gittin' ashore may do him good. You see, bein' the only doctor in the ship, he couldn't attend to hisself as well as might be, mayhap."

While Joe and Otto were conversing, the first boat load of emigrants landed, consisting chiefly of women and children. Dr Marsh was also among them, in order that, as he said with quiet pleasantry, he might attend to the sanitary arrangements of the camp in the new land, though all who saw him quit the wreck were under the sorrowful impression that the new land would prove to be in his case a last resting-place.

There was something peculiarly attractive in the manly, handsome face of this young disciple of Aesculapius, worn as it was by long sickness and suffering, and Otto fell in love with him at first sight.

There can be no doubt that some human beings are so constituted as to powerfully attract others by their mere physical conformation and expression, without reference to character or conduct,—indeed, before character or conduct can possibly be known. And when this peculiar conformation and expression is coupled with delicacy of health, and obvious suffering, the attractive influence becomes irresistible. Let us thank God that such is the case. Blind, unreasoning affection is a grand foundation on which to build a mighty superstructure of good offices, kindly acts, and tender feelings, mingled, it may be, with loving forbearance, and occasional suffering, which shall be good to the souls of the lover, as well as the loved one.

Anyhow, when Otto saw Dr Marsh helped, almost lifted, out of the boat; observed him give a pitiful little smile, and heard him utter some mild pleasantry to those who assisted him, he experienced a gush of feeling such as had never before inflated his reckless little bosom, and something like water— to his great astonishment—caused interference with his vision.

Running forward just as the widow Lynch was officiously thrusting her warm-hearted attentions on the invalid, he accosted the doctor, and offered to escort him to the golden cave.

And we may here inform the reader that the involuntary affection of our little hero met with a suitable return, for Dr Marsh also fell in love with Otto at first sight. His feelings, however, were strongly mingled with surprise.

"My boy," he said, with painfully wide-open eyes, "from what part of the sky have *you* dropt?"

"Well, not being a falling star or a rocket-stick, I cannot claim such high descent,—but hasn't the mate told you about us?" returned Otto.

Here widow Lynch broke in with:

"Towld him about you? Av course he hasn't. He don't throuble his hid to tell much to any wan; an', sure, wasn't the doctor slaapin' whin he returned aboord i' the night, an' wasn't I nursin' of 'im, and d'ee think any wan could git at 'im widout my lave?"

Otto thought that certainly no one could easily accomplish that feat, and was about to say so, when Dr Marsh said remonstratively—

"Now, my dear widow Lynch, do leave me to the care of this new friend, who, I am sure, is quite able to assist me, and do you go and look after these poor women and children. They are quite helpless without your aid. Look! your favourite Brown-eyes will be in the water if you don't run."

The child of a poor widow, which had been styled Brown-eyes by the doctor because of its gorgeous optics, was indeed on the point of taking an involuntary bath as he spoke. Mrs Lynch, seeing the danger, rushed tumultuously to the rescue, leaving the doctor to Otto's care.

"Don't let me lean too heavily on you," he said, looking down; "I'm big-boned, you see, and long-legged, though rather thin."

"Pooh!" said Otto, looking up, "you're as light as a feather, and I'm as strong as a horse,—a little horse, at least. You'd better not go to the camp yet, they are not ready for you, and that sweet little delicate creature you call widow Lynch is

R. M. Ballantyne

quite able to manage them all. Come up with me to the cave. But has nobody said a word about *us*?"

"Not a soul. As the widow told you, I was asleep when the mate returned to the wreck. Indeed, it is not very long since I awoke. I did hear some mention in passing of a few people being on the island, but I thought they referred to savages."

"Perhaps they were not far wrong," said Otto, with a laugh. "I do feel pretty savage sometimes, and Dominick is awful when he is roused; but we can't count Pauline among the savages."

"Dominick! Pauline!" exclaimed the doctor. "My good fellow, explain yourself, and let us sit down on this bank while you do so. I'm so stupidly weak that walking only a few yards knocks me up."

"Well, only two or three yards further will bring you to our cave, which is just beyond that cluster of bushes, but it may be as well to enlighten you a little before introducing you."

In a few rapid sentences Otto explained their circumstances, and how they came to be there. He told his brief tale in sympathetic ears.

"And your own name," asked the doctor, "is—?"

"Otto Rigonda."

"Well, Otto, my boy, you and I shall be friends; I know it—I feel it."

"And I'm *sure* of it," responded the enthusiastic boy, grasping the hand of the invalid, and shaking it almost too warmly. "But come, I want to present you to my sister.

Dominick is already among the emigrants, for I saw him leave the cave and go down to the camp when you were disputing with that female grampus."

"Come, don't begin our friendship by speaking disrespectfully of one of my best friends," said the doctor, rising; "but for widow Lynch's tender nursing I don't think I should be here now."

"I'll respect and reverence her henceforth and for ever," said Otto. "But here we are—this is the golden cave. Now you'll have to stoop, because our door was made for short men like me—and for humble long ones like my brother."

"I'll try to be a humble long one," said the doctor as he stooped and followed Otto into the cave.

Pauline was on her knees in front of the fire, with her back to the door, as they entered. She was stooping low and blowing at the flames vigorously.

"O Otto!" she exclaimed, without looking round, "this fire will break my heart. It *won't* light!"

"More company, Pina," said her brother.

Pauline sprang up and turned round with flushed countenance and disordered hair; and again Otto had the ineffable delight of seeing human beings suddenly reduced to that condition which is variously described as being "stunned," "thunderstruck," "petrified," and "struck all of a heap" with surprise.

Pauline was the first to recover self-possession.

"Really, Otto, it is too bad of you to take one by surprise so.

Excuse me, sir,—no doubt you are one of the unfortunates who have been wrecked. I have much pleasure in offering you the hospitality of our humble home!"

Pauline spoke at first half jestingly, but when she looked full at the thin, worn countenance of the youth who stood speechless before her, she forgot surprise and everything else in a feeling of pity.

"But you have been ill," she continued, sympathetically; "this wreck must have—pray sit down."

She placed a little stool for her visitor beside the fire.

If Dr John Marsh had spoken the words that sprang to his lips he would have begun with "Angelic creature," but he suppressed his feelings and only stammered—

"Your b-brother, Miss Rigonda, must have a taste for taking people by surprise, for he did not tell me that—that—I—I mean he did not prepare me for—for—you are right. I think I had better sit down, for I have, as you perceive, been very ill, and am rather weak, and—and in the circumstances such an unexpected—a—"

At this critical moment Dominick fortunately entered the cave, and rescued the doctor from the quicksand, in which he was floundering.

"Oh! you must be the very man I want," he said, grasping his visitor by the hand.

"That is strange," returned the doctor, with a languid smile, "seeing that you have never met me before."

"True, my good sir; nevertheless I may venture to say that I know you well, for there's a termagant of an Irish woman down at the camp going about wringing her hands, shouting out your good qualities in the most pathetic tones, and giving nobody a moment's peace because she does not know what has become of you. Having a suspicion that my brother must have found you and brought you here, I came to see. But pray, may I ask your name, for the Irish woman only describes you as 'Doctor, dear!'"

"Allow me to introduce him," cried Otto, "as an old friend of mine—Dr Marsh."

Dominick looked at his brother in surprise.

"Otto is right," said the doctor, with a laugh, "at least if feeling may be permitted to do duty for time in gauging the friendship."

"Well, Dr Marsh, we are happy to make your acquaintance, despite the sadness of the circumstances," said Dominick, "and will do all we can for you and your friends; meanwhile, may I ask you to come to the camp and relieve the mind of your worshipper, for I can scarcely call her less."

Poor Dr Marsh, feeling greatly exhausted by excitement as much as by exertion, was on the point of excusing himself and begging his host to fetch the widow up to the cave, when he was saved the trouble by the widow herself, whose voice was just then heard outside.

"What's that yer sayin', Joe?" she exclaimed in a remonstrative tone, "ye seed 'im go into that rabbit-hole? Never! Don't tell me! Arrah it's on his hands an knees he'd have to do it."

The voice which replied was pitched in a much deeper and

softer key, but it was heard distinctly to say, "Ay, widdy Lynch, that's the door I seed him an' a boy go through; so ye'd better rap at it an' inquire."

"Faix, an' that's jist what I'll do, though I don't half belave ye."

She was about to apply her large red knuckles to the door in question when her intention was frustrated and her doubts were scattered by the door opening and Dominick presenting himself.

"Come in, Mrs Lynch, come in. Your doctor is here, alive and well."

"Well, is it—ah! I wish he was! Are ye there, darlin'?"

"Yes, yes," came from within, in a laughing voice. "Here I am, Mrs Lynch, all right and comfortable. Come in."

Being excessively tall, the widow was obliged, like others, to stoop to enter; but being also excessively broad, she only got her head and shoulders through the doorway, and then, unlike others, she stuck fast. By dint, however, of a good pull from Dominick and a gentle push from Joe, she was got inside without quite carrying away the structure which the gale of the preceding night had spared.

"Och! 'tis a quare place intirely, and there is some disadvantage in bein' big—thank ye kindly, sir—but on the whole—"

She got no further, for at that moment her sharp little grey eyes fell on Pauline, and once again Otto's heart was stirred to its profoundest depths by the expressive glare that ensued. Indeed, Dominick and Marsh were equally affected, and could not help laughing.

"Ha! ye may laugh," said the widow, with profound solemnity, "but if it's not dramin' I am, what Father Macgrath says about ghosts is true, and—"

"I hope you don't take *me* for a ghost, Mrs Lynch," said Pauline, stepping forward with a kindly smile and holding out her hand.

"No, cushla! I don't," returned the widow, accepting the hand tenderly. "Sure it's more like a ghost the doctor is, in spite of his larfin'. But wonders 'll niver cease. I'll lave 'im wid an aisy mind, for he's in good hands. Now, Joe, clear out o' the door, like a good man, an' let me through. They'll be wantin' me at the camp. A good haul, Joe, I'm tough; no fear o' me comin' to pieces. Och! but it's a poor cabin. An Irish pig wouldn't thank ye for it."

Murmuring similar uncomplimentary remarks, mingled with expressions of surprise, the voice of the woman gradually died away, and the people in the golden cave were left to discuss their situation and form hasty plans for the present emergency.

At first, of course, they could do little else than make each other partially acquainted with the circumstances which had so strangely thrown them together, but Dominick soon put an end to this desultory talk.

"You see, it will take all our time," he said, "between this and sunset to get the emigrants comfortably under canvas, or some sort of shelter."

"True," assented Dr Marsh, "and it would never do with so many women and children, some of whom are on the sick

R. M. Ballantyne

list, to leave them to the risk of exposure to another storm like that which has just passed. Is your island subject to such?"

"By no means," answered Dominick. "It has a splendid climate. This gale is quite exceptional. Nevertheless, we cannot tell when the next may burst on us. Come, Otto, you and I will go down to the camp. Now, Dr Marsh, you must remain here. I can see, without being told, that you are quite unfit to help us. I know that it is hard to be condemned to inaction when all around are busy, but reflect how many patients you have solemnly warned that their recovery would depend on implicit obedience to the doctor's orders! Divide yourself in two, now, and, as a doctor, give yourself strict orders to remain quiet."

"H'm! Gladly would I divide myself," was the doctor's reply, "if while I left the patient half to act the invalid, I could take the impatient half down to the camp to aid you. But I submit. The days of my once boasted strength are gone. I feel more helpless than a mouse."

There was something quite pitiful in the half-humorous look, and the weary sigh, with which the poor youth concluded his remarks, and Otto was so touched that he suddenly suggested the propriety of his staying behind and taking care of him.

"Why, you conceited creature," cried Dominick, "of what use could *you* be? Besides, don't you think that Pina is a sufficiently good nurse?"

Otto humbly admitted that she was.

Dr Marsh, glancing at her pretty face, on which at the moment there beamed an expression of deep sympathy, also admitted that she was; but, being a man of comparatively few words, he said nothing.

It was a busy day for Dominick and his brother. Not only had they to counsel and advise with the unfortunate emigrants as to the best position for the temporary encampment, with reference to wood and water, as well as to assist with their own hands in the erection of tents made of torn sails and huts and booths composed of broken planks and reeds, but they had to answer innumerable questions from the inquisitive as to their own history, from the anxious as to the probabilities of deliverance, from the practical as to the resources of the islands, and from the idiotic as to everything in general and nothing in particular. In addition to which they had to encourage the timid, to correct the mistaken, and to remonstrate with or resist the obstinate; also to romp a little with the children as they recovered their spirits, quiet the babies as they recovered their powers of lung, and do a little amateur doctoring for the sick in the absence of the medical man.

In all these varied occupations they were much aided by the widow Lynch, who, instead of proving to be, as they had expected, a troublesome termagant, turned out to be a soft-hearted, kindly, enthusiastic, sympathetic woman, with a highly uneducated, unbalanced mind, a powerfully consti-tuted and masculine frame, and "a will of her own." In this last particular she did not differ much from the rest of the human species, but she was afflicted with an unusually strong desire to assert it.

Very like Mrs Lynch in the matters of kindly soft-heartedness and sympathy was Mrs Welsh—a poor, gentle, delicate Englishwoman, the wife of a great hulking cross-grained fellow named Abel, who was a carpenter by trade and an idler by preference. Mrs Welsh was particularly good as a sick-nurse and a cook, in which capacities she made herself extremely useful.

About midday, Mrs Welsh having prepared a glorious though simple meal for her section of the emigrant band, and the other sections having been ministered to more or less successfully by their more or less capable cooks, Dominick and Otto went up to the golden cave to dinner, which they well knew the faithful Pauline would have ready waiting for them.

"What a day we have had, to be sure!" said Dominick as they walked along; "and I'm as hungry as a kangaroo."

Without noticing the unreasonableness of supposing that long-legged creature to be the hungriest of animals, Otto declared that he was in the same condition, "if not more so."

On opening the door they were checked by the expression of Pauline's face, the speaking eyes of which, and the silent mouth, were concentrated into an unmistakable "hush!"—which was emphasised by a significant forefinger.

"What's wrong?" whispered Dominick, anxiously.

"Sleeping," murmured Pauline—she was too good a nurse to whisper—pointing to the invalid, who, overcome with the night's exposure and the morning's excitement, had fallen into a profound slumber on Otto's humble couch.

This was a rather severe and unexpected trial to Otto, who had come up to the cave brimming over with camp news for Pauline's benefit. He felt that it was next to impossible to relate in a whisper all the doings and sayings, comical and otherwise, that he had seen and heard that day. To eat his dinner and say nothing seemed equally impossible. To awaken the wearied sleeper was out of the question.

However, there was nothing for it but to address himself to the suppression of his feelings. Probably it was good for him to be thus self-disciplined; certainly it was painful.

He suffered chiefly at the top of the nose—inside behind his eyes—that being the part of the safety-valve where bursts of laughter were checked; and more than once, while engaged in a whispering commentary on the amiable widow Lynch, the convulsions within bade fair to blow the nasal organ off his face altogether. Laughter is catching. Pauline and Dominick, ere long, began to wish that Otto would hold his tongue. At last, some eccentricity of Joe Binney, or his brother, or Mrs Lynch, we forget which, raised the pressure to such a pitch that the safety-valves of all three became ineffective. They all exploded in unison, and poor Marsh was brought to consciousness, surprise, and a sitting posture at the same instant.

"I'm afraid," he said, rather sheepishly, "that I've been sleeping."

"You have, doctor, and a right good sleep you've had," said Dominick, rising and placing a stool for the invalid. "We ought to apologise for disturbing you; but come, sit down and dine. You must be hungry by this time."

"Indeed I am. The land air seems to have had a powerful effect on me already."

"Truly it must," remarked Pauline, "else you could not have fallen asleep in the very middle of my glowing description of our island home."

"Did I really do that?" said the doctor, with an air of self-reproach.

"Indeed you did; but in the circumstances you are to be excused."

"And I hope," added Dominick, "that you'll have many a good sleep in our golden cave."

"Golden cave, indeed," echoed the invalid, in thought, for his mind was too much taken up just then with Pauline to find vent in speech. "A golden cave it will be to me for evermore!"

It is of no use mincing the matter; Dr John Marsh, after being regarded by his friends at home as hopelessly unimpressible —in short, an absolute woman-hater—had found his fate on a desolate isle of the Southern seas, he had fallen—nay, let us be just—had jumped over head and ears in love with Pauline Rigonda! Dr Marsh was no sentimental die-away noodle who, half-ashamed, half-proud of his condition, displays it to the semi-contemptuous world. No; after disbelieving for many years in the power of woman to subdue him, he suddenly and manfully gave in—sprang up high into the air, spiritually, and so to speak, turning a sharp somersault, went headlong down deep into the flood, without the slightest intention of ever again returning to the surface.

But of this mighty upheaval and overturning of his sentiments he betrayed no symptom whatever, excepting two bright spots—one on either cheek—which might easily have been mistaken for the effects of weakness, or recent excitement, or bad health, or returning hunger. Calmly he set to work on the viands before him with unusual appetite, conversing earnestly, meanwhile, with Dominick and Otto on the gravity of their situation, and bestowing no more attention upon Pauline than was barely consistent with good breeding, insomuch that that pretty young creature began to feel somewhat aggrieved. Considering all the care she had so recently bestowed on him, she came to the conclusion, in short, that he was by no means as polite as at first she had supposed him to be.

By degrees the conversation about the present began to give place to discussions as to the future, and when Dominick and Otto returned for their evening meal at sunset, bringing with them Mr Malines, the mate, and Joe Binney and his brother David and Hugh Morris as being representative men of the emigrants and ship's crew, the meeting resolved itself into a regular debating society. At this point Pauline deserted them and went down to the camp to cultivate the acquaintance of the widow Lynch, Mrs Welsh, and the other female and infantine members of the wrecked party.

"For my part," said Malines, "I shall take one o' the boats, launch it in the lagoon, and go over to the big island, follow me who may, for it is clear that there's not room for us all on this strip of sand."

"I don't see that," objected Hugh Morris. "Seems to me as there's space enough for all of us, if we're not too greedy."

"That shows ye knows nothin' about land, Hugh," said Joe Binney. "What's of it here is not only too little, but too sandy. I votes for the big island."

"So does I," said David Binney. "Big Island for me."

Thus, incidentally, was the large island named.

"But," said Hugh, still objecting, "it won't be half so convenient to git things out o' the wreck, as where we are."

"Pooh! that's nothing," said Malines. "It won't cost us much trouble to carry all we want across a spit of sand."

Seeing that the two men were getting angry with each other, Dominick interposed by blandly stating that he knew well the capabilities of the spot on which they were encamped, and he was sure that such a party would require more ground if they meant to settle on it.

"Well now, master," observed Joe, with a half-laugh, "we don't 'zactly mean for to settle on it, but here we be, an' here we must be, till a ship takes us off, an' we can't afford to starve, 'ee know, so we'll just plough the land an' plant our seed, an' hope for good weather an' heavy crops; so I says Big Island!"

"An' so says I—Big Island for ever!" repeated his brother David.

After a good deal more talk and altercation this was finally agreed to, and the meeting dissolved itself.

That night, at the darkest hour, another meeting was held in the darkest spot that could be found near the camp. It chanced, unknown to the meeting, to be the burial-ground at first discovered by the Rigondas.

Unwittingly, for it was very dark, Hugh Morris seated himself on one of the old graves, and about thirty like-minded men gathered round him. Little did they know that Otto was one of the party! Our little hero, being sharp eyed and eared, had seen and overheard enough in the camp that day to induce him to watch Morris after he left the cave, and follow him to the rendezvous.

"My lads," said Morris, "I've done my best to keep them to the reef, but that blackguard Malines won't hear of it. He's bent on takin' 'em all to the big island, so they're sure to go, and we won't get the help o' the other men: but no matter; wi' blocks an' tackle we'll do it ourselves, so we can afford to remain quiet till our opportunity comes. I'm quite sure the ship lays in such a position that we can get her over the ledge into deep water, and so be able to draw round into the open sea, and then—"

"Hurrah for the black flag and the southern seas," cried one of the party.

"No, no, Jabez Jenkins," said Morris, "we don't mean to be pirates; only free rovers."

"Hallo! what's this?" exclaimed another of the party. "A cross, I do believe! and this mound—why, it's a grave!"

"And here's another one!" said Jabez, in a hoarse whisper. "Seems to me we've got into a cannibal churchyard, or—"

"Bo-o-o-o-oo!" groaned Otto at that moment, in the most horribly sepulchral tone he could command.

Nothing more was wanted. With one consent the conspirators leapt up and fled from the dreadful spot in a frenzy of unutterable consternation.

R. M. Ballantyne

CHAPTER SEVEN

TREATS OF BIG ISLAND—A GREAT FIGHT
AND A ROYAL FAMILY

"Dominick," said Otto, next morning, after having solemnly and somewhat mysteriously led his brother to the old burial-ground, "would you believe me if I told you that last night, when you and the like of you were sound asleep, not to say snoring, I saw some twenty or thirty men fly from this spot like maniacs at the howling of a ghost?"

"No, I would not believe you," answered Dominick, with a bland smile.

"Would you not believe me if I told you that *I* was the ghost and that Hugh Morris was the ringleader of the cowards?"

"Come, Otto, be sensible and explain."

Otto became sensible and explained. Thereupon Dominick became serious, and said "Oho!" To which Otto replied "Just so," after which they became meditative. Then Dominick linked his arm in that of his little brother, and, leading him off to a well-known and sequestered walk, entered into an earnest confabulation.

With the details of that confabulation we will not trouble the reader. We will only repeat the concluding sentences.

"Well, then, Dom, it's agreed on, that we are to go on as if we knew nothing about this matter, and take no notice of it whatever to any one—not even to Pina."

"Yes, Otto, that's it. Of course I don't like to have any sort of secret from Pina, but it would be cruel in us to fill her mind with alarm for no good purpose. No—mum's the word. Take no notice whatever. Morris may repent. Give him the benefit of the doubt, or the hope."

"Very well, Dom, mum shall be the word."

Having thus for the time being disposed of a troublesome subject, the brothers returned to the place where the emigrants were encamped.

Here all was wild confusion and harmony. Lest this should appear contradictory, we must explain that the confusion was only physical, and addressed to the eye. The emigrants, who were busy as ants, had already disembarked large quantities of their goods, which were scattered about in various heaps between the landing-place and the encampment. The harmony, on the other hand, was mental and spiritual, for as yet there had been no time for conflicting interests to arise, and the people were all so busy that they had not leisure to disagree.

Besides, the weather being splendidly bright and warm was conducive to good-humour. It will be remembered also that Hugh Morris and his friends had resolved to remain quiet for the present. Perhaps the effect of the ghostly visitation might have had some influence in restraining their turbulent spirits.

At all events, be this as it may, when Dominick and Otto came upon the scene everything was progressing pleasantly. The male emigrants were running between the beach and the camp with heavy burdens on their shoulders. The females were busy washing and mending garments, which stood sorely in need of their attention, or tending the sick and what Otto styled the infantry. The sailors were engaged, some in transporting goods from the wreck to the shore, others in piloting two of the large boats through the reef into the lagoon, and the larger children were romping joyously in the thickets and trying to climb the cocoa-nut trees, while the smaller fry were rolling helplessly on the sands—watched, more or less, by mothers and big sisters.

Chief among those who piloted the large boats through the passage in the reef was Hugh Morris. He took careful observations and soundings as he went along, not that such were needed for the safety of the boats, but Hugh Morris had an eye to the ultimate destiny of the ship.

"You're mighty particular, Morris," said Malines, with something of a sneer in his tone, when the former drew up his boat inside the reef beside the other boat. "One would think you were piloting a man-of-war through instead of a little boat."

"What I was doin' is none o' your business, Malines," returned Hugh, sternly. "Your command ceased when you lost your ship, and I ain't agoin' to obey your orders; no, nor take any of your cheek."

"The emigrants chose to accept me as their commander, at least for the present," retorted Malines, fiercely.

To this Hugh replied, with a laugh of scorn, that the emigrants might make a commander of the ship's monkey for all that he cared, the emigrants were not *his* masters, and he would do exactly as he pleased.

As a number of his followers echoed the scornful laugh, Malines felt that he had not the power to carry things with a high hand.

"Well, well," he returned, in a tone of quiet indifference, "we shall see. It is quite clear to every one with a grain of sense that people can't live comfortably under two masters; the people will have to decide that matter for themselves before long."

"Ay, that will they, master," remarked Joe Binney, in a low but significant voice. "Seems to me, however, that as we're all agreed about goin' over to Big Island, we'd better go about it an' leave disputation till afterwards."

Agreeing to this in silence, the men set about loading the boats for the first trip.

Dominick and Otto, standing on the beach, had witnessed this altercation.

"The seeds of much dissension and future trouble are there," remarked the former.

"Unless we prevent the growth of the seed," said Otto.

"True, but how that is to be done does not appear obvious at present. These men have strong wills and powerful frames, and each has a large following, I can see that. We must hope that among the emigrants there may be good and strong men enough to keep the crew in check."

"Luckily two of the biggest and stoutest are also the most

R. M. Ballantyne

sensible," said Otto.

"You mean the brothers Binney?"

"Yes, Dom. They're first-rate men, don't you think so?"

"Undoubtedly; but very ignorant, and evidently unaccustomed to lead or command men."

"What a pity," exclaimed the boy, with a flush of sudden inspiration, "that we couldn't make you king of the island! You're nearly as strong as the best of them, and much cleverer."

Dominick received this compliment with a laugh and a shake of the head.

"No, my boy; I am not nearly as strong as Malines or Morris, or the Binneys. Besides, you forget that 'the race is not always to the swift, nor the battle to the strong,' and as to cleverness, that does not consist in a superior education or a head crammed full of knowledge, but in the right and ready application of knowledge. No; I have no ambition to be a king. But it won't do for us to stand here talking, else we shall be set down as idlers. Come, let us lend a helping hand."

While the men were busy at the boats on the lagoon side of the reef, Pauline was winning golden opinions among the women at the camp by the hearty, unaffected way in which she went about making herself generally useful. O blessed simplicity, how adorable art thou in man and woman! Self-forgetfulness was a salient point in Pauline's character, and, being conjoined with strong powers of sympathy, active good-will to man and beast, and more than the average of intellectual capacity, with an under-current of rippling fun, the girl's influence quickly made itself felt.

Mrs Lynch said she was a jewel, and that was extraordinary praise from the strapping widow, who seldom complimented her sex, whatever she may have felt. Mrs Welsh said she was a "dear, pritty creetur'," and laughter-loving little Mrs Nobbs, the wife of a jovial harum-scarum blacksmith, pronounced her a "perfect darling." As for the children, after one hour's acquaintance they adored her, and would have "bored her to death" had that been possible. What the men thought of her we cannot tell, for they spake not, but furtively stared at her in a sort of reverential amazement, and some of them, in a state of mild enthusiasm, gave murmured utterance to the sentence quoted above, "Blessed simplicity!" for Pauline Rigonda was, at first, utterly unaware of the sensation she created.

When the two boats were loaded down to the gunwales, a select party of men embarked and rowed them over the calm lagoon to Big Island. Of course they were well armed, for no one could tell what they might meet with there. Dominick and Otto were of the party, and, being regarded in some measure as owners of the soil, the former was tacitly recognised as leader on this their first visit.

The distance they had to row was not more than a quarter of a mile, so the lagoon was soon crossed. The spot at which they landed was a beautiful little bay with bush-topped cliffs on one side, a thicket of luxuriant plants on the other, and palm groves rising to a moderate height behind. The little beach on which they ran the boats was of pure white sand, which induced one of them to name it Silver Bay.

Jumping out, Dominick, with a dozen armed men, advanced into the bushes with caution.

"Nothing to be seen here of either friends or foes," he said, halting. "I felt sure that we should find no one, and it is of no use taking so many of you from work; therefore, lads, I would advise your returning to the boats and going to work at once. My little brother and I will ascend to the top of the cliff there, from which we will be able to see all the neighbouring country, and give you timely warning should any natives appear. Pile your rifles on the beach, so as to have them handy; but you've nothing to fear."

In a few minutes Dominick and his brother, each carrying a rifle and cutlass supplied by the wrecked party, had mounted to the top of the neighbouring cliff, while the men returned to aid in unloading the boats.

"What a splendid island!" exclaimed Otto, with intense delight, as, from the lofty outlook, they gazed down upon a scene of the richest beauty. From their position on the reef they had hitherto seen the island through the softening atmosphere of distance, like a rounded mass of verdure; but in this case distance had *not* "lent enchantment to the view," for, now that they beheld it spread in all its luxuriance at their feet, like a verdant gem resting on the breast of ocean, it appeared infinitely more beautiful. Not only was the mind charmed by the varied details of grove and bay, thicket and grotto, but the eye was attracted irresistibly to the magnificent trees and shrubs which stood prominent in their individuality—such as the light and elegant aito-tree; the stately apape, with its branchless trunk and light crown of pale green leaves, resembling those of the English ash; the splendid tamanu, an evergreen, with its laurel-shaped leaves; the imposing hutu-tree, with foliage resembling the magnolia and its large white flowers, the petals of which are edged with bright pink;—these and many others, with the feathery palm and several kinds of mimosa lining the seashore, presented a display of form and colour such as the brothers had not up to that time even dreamed of.

While Otto gazed in silent wonder and admiration, he was surprised to hear Dominick give vent to a sigh, and shake his head.

"Dom!" he said, remonstratively, "what do you mean by that?"

"I mean that the place is such a paradise that the emigrants won't want to leave it, and that will interfere with a little plan which had begun to form itself in my brain of late. I had been thinking that among so many tradesmen I should find men to help me to break up the wreck, and, out of the materials, to build a small vessel, with which to leave the island—for, to tell you the truth, Otto, I have begun to fear that this place lies so far out of the track of ships that we may be left on it for many years like the mutineers of Pitcairn Island."

"Humph! I'm sorry you're growing tired of it already," said Otto; "I thought you had more o' the spirit of Robinson Crusoe in you, Dom, and I never heard of the mutineers of Pitcairn Island; but if—"

"What! did you never hear of the mutineers of the *Bounty*?"

"Never. My education, you know, has been neglected."

"Then I'll tell you the story some time or other. It's too long to begin just now, but it beats that of your favourite Robinson out of sight in my opinion."

Otto shook his head in grave unbelief. "That," he said, "is impossible. But as to this island proving so attractive, don't you think that such fellows as Hugh Morris and Malines will take care to prevent it becoming too much of a paradise?"

Dominick laughingly admitted that there was something in that—and he was right. There was even more in that than he had imagined, for the party had not been a week in their new home when they began to differ as to the division of the island. That old, old story of mighty men desiring to take possession of the land and push their weaker brethren to the wall soon began to be re-enacted on this gem of the ocean, and bade fair to convert the paradise—like the celebrated Monte Carlo—into a magnificent pandemonium.

At one of their stormy meetings, of which the settlers had many, the brothers Binney and Dominick were present. It was held on the shores of Silver Bay, where the first boat-loads had been discharged, and around which quite a village of rude huts had sprung up like mushrooms. From those disputatious assemblies most of the women absented themselves, but the widow Lynch always remained, holding herself in reserve for any emergency, for she was well aware that her opinion carried much weight with many of the party.

"We're a rough lot, and would need tight handlin'," whispered the little man named Redding to Joe Binney, who sat on a bank beside him.

"The handlin' will be tight enough before long," returned Joe, with a decided little nod. "Listen, the worst o' the lot's agoin' to spout."

This last remark had reference to Malines, who had just risen to reply to a fiery little man named Buxley, a tailor by trade, who was possessed not only of good reasoning power but great animal courage, as he had proved on more than one occasion on the voyage out.

"Friends," said the mate, "it's all very well for Buxley to talk about fair play, and equal rights, etcetera, but, I ask, would it be fair play to give each of us an equal portion of land, when it's quite clear that some—like Joe Binney there—could cultivate twice as much as his share, while a creature like Buxley—"

"No more a creature than yourself!" shouted the little tailor.

"Could only work up half his lot—if even so much," continued the mate, regardless of the interruption.

"Hear, hear!" from those who sympathised with Malines.

"An' what could *you* do with land?" demanded Buxley in a tone of scorn, "a man that's ploughed nothing but salt water all his life."

This was greeted with a laugh and "That's so." "He's only sowed wild oats as yet." "Pitch into him, Buckie."

Malines was fast losing temper under the little man's caustic remarks, but succeeded in restraining himself, and went on:—

"It's quite plain that the island is too small to let every man have an equal bit of land, so I propose that it should be divided among those who have strength and knowledge to work it, and—"

"*You* ain't one o' them," shouted the irate tailor.

"Come, come, Buxley—let him speak," said Joe Binney, "fair play, ye know. That's what you sticks up for, ain't it? Let 'im speak."

R. M. Ballantyne

"Anyhow," continued Malines, sharply, "*I* mean to keep the bit o' ground I've staked off whether you like it or no—"

"An' so do I," cried Welsh, who was what may be styled a growly man.

"Sure, an' so does myself," said Teddy Malone, "for I've staked off a bit about six feet long an' two broad, to plant mesilf in whin I give up the ghost."

This mild pleasantry seemed to calm a little the rising wrath of contending parties, much to Dominick's satisfaction, for he was exceedingly anxious to keep in the background and avoid interference. During the week that had passed, he had more than once been forced to have sharp words with Malines, and felt that if he was to act as a peacemaker— which he earnestly wished to do—he must avoid quarrelling with him if possible.

The hopes of those who wished to settle matters amicably, however, were dashed by the fiery tailor, who, still smarting under the contemptuous tones and words of the mate, suddenly sprang to his feet and suggested that, as Malines knew nothing about agriculture, no land at all should be apportioned to him, but that he should be set to fishing, or some such dirty work, for the benefit of the community.

This was too much for Malines, who strode towards Buxley with clenched fists and furious looks, evidently intending to knock him down. To the surprise and amusement of every one, Buxley threw himself into a pugilistic attitude, and shouted defiantly, "Come on!" There is no saying how the thing would have ended, if Dominick had not quickly interposed.

"Come, Mr Malines," he said, "it is not very creditable in

you to threaten a man so very much smaller than yourself."

"Out of my road," shouted the mate, fiercely, "we don't want *gentlemen* to lord it over us."

"No, nor yet *blackguards*," growled a voice in the crowd.

This so angered Malines, that he dealt Dominick a sounding slap on the cheek.

For a moment there was dead silence, as the two men glared at each other. If it had been a blow the youth might have stood it better, but there was something so stinging, as well as insulting, in a slap, that for a moment he felt as if his chest would explode. Before he could act, however, Joe Binney thrust his bulky form between the men.

"Leave'm to me, master," he said, quietly turning up his wristbands, "I'm used to this sort o' thing, an'—"

"No, no," said Dominick, in a deep, decided voice, "listen."

He grasped Joe by the arm, and whispered a few words in his ear. A smile broke over the man's face, and he shook his head doubtfully.

"Well, it may be so," he remarked, "an' no doubt it would have a good effect."

"Now, then, stand aside," said Dominick, as he retreated a few paces and threw off his coat, while Malines still stood in a threatening attitude, with an expression of contempt on his face. "My friends," he said, as he slowly rolled up his shirt-sleeves, showing a pair of arms which, although not bulky, displayed an amount of sinews and muscle that was suggestive of knotted ropes under a fair skin—

R. M. Ballantyne

"My friends," he said, "somewhere in the Bible it is written, 'Smite a scorner, and the simple will beware.' I have done my best to conciliate *this* scorner without success; I shall now try to smite him."

"An' brother David an' me will see fair play," remarked Joe Binney.

If the combatants had been more equally matched, the spectators would probably have encouraged Dominick with a cheer, but the difference in size was so apparent, that astonishment kept them silent. Dominick was indeed fully as tall as his opponent, and his shoulders were nearly as broad, but the massive weight of Malines's figure seemed to render the chance of Dominick's success highly improbable.

The youth sprang at him, however, like lightning, and, hitting him a violent blow on the forehead, leapt back out of his reach.

The blow had the effect that was intended; it roused the mate's wrath to the utmost pitch, causing him to rush at his opponent, striking right and left with all his force. Dominick, however, leapt about with such activity, that only a few of the blows reached him, and these not with their full force. The result was that the mate became what is styled winded in a few minutes, and was compelled to pause to recover himself, but Dominick had no intention of allowing him time to recover himself. Without a moment's hesitation, he sprang in again and planted a severe left-hander between his opponent's eyes. This roused the mate once more to white heat, and he sought to close with his foe, but the latter prevented that by leaping aside, tripping him up, and causing him to plunge forward on his hands and knees—assisting him to that position with a stiff rap on the right temple as he passed.

Then it was that Malines discovered that he had drawn on himself the wrath of one who had been the champion boxer in a large public school, and was quite as tough as himself in wind and limb, though not so strong or so heavy.

Now, it is not our intention to give a graphic account of that pugilistic encounter. Yet is it needful to point out briefly how, being a man of peace, as well as a man of science, Dominick managed to bring this fight to as speedy a close as possible. Instead, then, of striking his foe in all directions, and producing a disgusting scene of bloodshed, he confined his practice chiefly to one spot, between the eyes, close above the bridge of the nose—varying it a little with a shot now and then under each eye. This had the effect, owing to constant repetition, of gradually shutting up both Malines's eyes so that he could not easily see. When in this condition, Dominick suddenly delivered first a left and then a right hander into what is sometimes called the breadbasket, and stretched his adversary on the sand.

Dominick was not boastful or ungenerous. He did not crow over his fallen foe. On the contrary, he offered to assist that smitten scorner to rise, but Malines preferred in the meantime to lie still.

It is scarcely necessary to say that the emigrants watched this short but sharp encounter with keen interest, and when it was ended gave vent to a cheer, in which surprise was quite as clearly expressed as satisfaction.

"Now, I tell 'ee what it is, lads," said Joe Binney, striking his great right fist into the palm of his left hand enthusiastically, "I never seed the likes o' that since I was a leetle booy, and I've got a motion for to propose, as they say at meetin's. It's this, that we makes Master Dom'nik Riggundy capting over us all."

Up started Teddy Malone, with a slap of his thigh. "And it's mesilf as'll second that motion—only we should make him governor of the whole island, if not king!"

"Hear! hear!" shouted a decided majority of the party. "Let him be king!"

When silence had been partially restored Dominick politely but firmly declined the honour, giving it as his opinion that the fairest way would be to have a republic.

"A republic! No; what we wants is a despotism," said David Binney, who had up to this point remained silent, "a regular despot—a howtocrat—is what we wants to keep us in order."

"Hump!" exclaimed Hugh Morris, contemptuously, "if you'd on'y let Malines have his way you'd soon have a despot an' a howtocrat as 'ud keep yer noses to the grindstone."

"Mrs Lynch," whispered Otto, who had hitherto stood beside the widow watching the proceedings with inexpressible glee, "you get up an' propose that Pina should be *queen!*"

That this suggestion came upon the widow with a shock of surprise, as well as approval, was obvious from the wide-eyed stare, with which for a moment she regarded the boy, and from her subsequent action. Taking a bold and masculine stride to the front of the disputers, she turned about and faced them.

"Howld yer tongues now, boys, all of you, and listen to what your grandmother's got to say."

A shout of laughter cut her short for a few seconds.

"That's right, old 'ooman, out with it."

"Sure, if ye'd stop your noise I'd out wid it fast enough. Now, then, here ye are, nivver a man of ye able to agree wid the others; an' the raisin's not far to seek—for yer all wrong together. It would nivver do to make wan o' you a king—not even Joe here, for he knows nixt to nothin', nor yet Mister Rig Gundy, though he can fight like a man, for it's not a king's business to fight. No, take my word for it; what ye want is a *queen*—"

A loud explosion of mirth drowned the rest. "Hurrah! for Queen Lynch," cried one. "The Royal blood of owld Ireland for ivver!" shouted Malone.

"I wouldn't," said the widow indignantly, "condescind to reign over sitch a nation o' pigs, av ye was to go down on yer bare knees an' scrape them to the bone. No, it's English blood, or Spanitch, I don't rightly know which, that I'm drivin' at, for where could ye find a better, or honester, or purtier queen than that swate creetur, Miss Pauline Rig Gundy?"

The idea seemed to break upon the assembly as a light in a dark place. For a moment they seemed struck dumb; then there burst forth such a cheer as showed that the greater part of those present sympathised heartily with the proposal.

"I know'd ye'd agree to it. Sure, men always does when a sensible woman spakes. You see, Queen Pauline the First—"

"Hurrah! for Queen Pauline the First," yelled the settlers, with mingled cheers and laughter.

"Queen Pauline the First, ye may be sure," continued the widow, "would nivver try to kape order wid her fists, nor yit wid shoutin' or swearin'. An' then, av coorse, it would be aisy to make Mister Duminick or Joe Binney Prime Minister, an' little Buxley Chancler o' the Checkers, or whatever they calls it. Now, think over it, boys, an' good luck be wid ye."

They did think over it, then and there, in real earnest, and the possibility of an innocent, sensible, gentle, just, sympathetic, and high-minded queen reigning over them proved so captivating to these rough fellows, that the idea which had been at first received in jest crystallised into a serious purpose. At this point Otto ventured to raise his voice in this first deliberation of the embryo State.

"Friends," he said, with an air of modesty, which, we fear, was foreign to his nature, "although I can only appear before you as a boy, my big brother has this day proved himself to be so much more than an ordinary man that I feel somehow as if I had a right to his surplus manhood, being next-of-kin, and therefore I venture to address you as a sort of man." (Hear, hear!) "I merely wish to ask a question. May I ask to be the bearer of the news of this assembly's determination to—the—the *Queen*?"

"Yes—yes—of course—av course," were the immediate replies.

Otto waited not for more, but sped to their new hut, in which the Queen was busy preparing dinner at the time.

"Pina," exclaimed the boy, bursting in, "will you consent to be the Queen of Big Island?"

"Come, Otto; don't talk nonsense. I hope Dom is with you. Dinner is much overdone already."

"No, but I'm not talking nonsense," cried Otto. "I say, will you consent to be a queen—a *real* queen—Pina the First, eh?"

Hereupon he gave his wondering sister a graphic account of the recent meeting, and fight, and final decision.

"But they don't really mean it, you know," said Pauline, laughing.

"But they do really mean it," returned Otto; "and, by the way, if *you* become a queen won't that necessarily make me and Dom princes?"

As Dominick entered the hut at that moment he joined in the laugh which this question created, and corroborated his brother's statement.

In this cheerful frame of mind the new Royal Family sat down to dinner.

R. M. Ballantyne

CHAPTER EIGHT

THE CORONATION—CROWN-MAKING DELIBERATIONS, CEREMONIALS, AND CATASTROPHES

There came a day, not many weeks later in the history of our emigrants, when great preparations were made for an important and unusual event.

This was neither more nor less than the coronation of Queen Pauline the First.

The great event had been delayed by the unfortunate illness of the elect queen herself—an illness brought on by reckless exposure in the pursuit of the picturesque and beautiful among the islets of the lagoon. In other words, Otto and she, when off on a fishing and sketching excursion in the dinghy of the wreck, had been caught in a storm and drenched to the skin. The result to Otto was an increase of appetite; to Pauline, a sharp attack of fever, which confined her for some time to the palace, as their little hut was now styled. Here the widow Lynch—acting the united parts of nurse, lady of the bedchamber, mistress of the robes, maid of honour, *chef de cuisine*, and any other office that the reader may recollect as belonging to royalty—did so conduct herself as to gain not only the approval but the affection and gratitude of her royal mistress.

During the period of Pauline's convalescence considerable changes had taken place in the circumstances and condition of the community. The mere fact that a government had been fixed on, the details of which were being wrought out by a committee of leading men appointed by the people, tended to keep the turbulent spirits pretty quiet, and enabled the well-disposed to devote all their strength of mind and body to the various duties that devolved upon them and the improving of their circumstances. Busy workers are usually peaceful. They have no time to quarrel. It is only when turbulent idlers interfere with or oppress them that the industrious are compelled to show their teeth and set up their backs.

During these weeks the appearance of the shores of Big Island began to change materially. All round the edge of Silver Bay a number of bright green patches were enclosed by rough but effective fences. These were the gardens of the community, in which sweet potatoes, yams, etcetera, grew spontaneously, while some vegetables of the northern hemisphere had already been sown, and were in some cases even beginning to show above ground. In these gardens, when the important work of planting had been finished, the people set about building huts of various shapes and sizes, according to their varying taste and capacity.

Even at this early stage in the life of the little community the difficulties which necessarily surround a state of civilisation began to appear, and came out at one of the frequent, though informal, meetings of the men on the sands of Silver Bay. It happened thus:—

It was evening. The younger and more lively men of the community, having a large store of surplus energy unexhausted after the labours of the day, began, as is the wont of the young and lively, to compete with one another in feats of agility and strength, while a group of their elders

R. M. Ballantyne

stood, sat, or reclined on a bank, discussing the affairs of the nation, and some of them enjoying their pipes—for, you see, everything in the wreck having been saved, they had, among other bad things, plenty of tobacco.

Dr Marsh sat among the elders, for, although several weeks on shore had greatly restored his health, he was still too weak to join in the athletics. A few of the women and children also looked on, but they stood aside by themselves, not feeling very much interested in the somewhat heated discussions of the men.

By degrees these discussions degenerated into disputes, and became at last so noisy that the young athletes were attracted, and some of them took part in the debates.

"I tell 'ee what it is," exclaimed Nobbs, the blacksmith, raising his powerful voice above the other voices, and lifting his huge fist in the air, "something'll have to be done, for I can't go on workin' for nothin' in this fashion."

"No more can I, or my mates," said Abel Welsh, the carpenter.

"Here comes the Prime Minister," cried Teddy Malone.

"To *be*—he ain't Prime Minister yet," growled Jabez Jenkins, who, being a secret ally of Hugh Morris, was one of the disaffected, and had, besides, a natural tendency to growl and object to everything.

"He *is* Prime Minister," cried the fiery little Buxley, starting up and extending his hand with the air of one who is about to make a speech. "No doubt the Queen ain't crowned yet, an' hasn't therefore appointed any one to be her Minister, but we know she means to do it and we're all agreed about it."

"No we ain't," interrupted Jenkins, angrily.

"Well, the most on us, then," retorted Buxley.

"Shut up, you radical!" said Nobbs, giving the tailor a facetious slap on the back, "an' let's hear what the Prime Minister himself has got to say about it."

"What is the subject under discussion?" inquired Dominick, who, with Otto, joined the group of men at the moment and flung down a basket of fine fish which he had just caught in the lagoon.

He turned to Dr Marsh for an answer.

"Do *you* explain your difficulties," said the doctor to the blacksmith.

"Well, sir," said Nobbs, "here's where it is. When I fust comed ashore an' set up my anvil an' bellows I went to work with a will, enjyin' the fun o' the thing an' the novelty of the sitivation; an' as we'd lots of iron of all kinds I knocked off nails an' hinges an' all sorts o' things for anybody as wanted 'em. Similarly, w'en Abel Welsh comed ashore he went to work with his mates at the pit-saw an' tossed off no end o' planks, etceterer. But you see, sir, arter a time we come for to find that we're workin' to the whole population for nothin', and while everybody else is working away at his own hut or garden, or what not, *our* gardens is left to work themselves, an' *our* huts is nowhere! Now, as we've got no money to pay for work with, and as stones an' shells won't answer the purpus—seein' there's a sight too much of 'em—the question is, what's to be done?"

"Not an easy question to answer, Nobbs," said Dominick, "and one that requires serious consideration. Perhaps, instead of trying to answer it at present, we might find a temporary expedient for the difficulty until a Committee of the House—if I may say so—shall investigate the whole problem." (Hear, hear from Malone, Redding, and Buxley, and a growl from Jenkins.) "I would suggest, then, in the meantime, that while Nobbs and Welsh,—who are, perhaps, the most useful men among us—continue to ply their trades for the benefit of the community, every man in the community shall in turn devote a small portion of time to working in the gardens and building the huts of these two men." (Hear, hear, from a great many of the hearers, and dissenting growls from a few.) "But," continued Dominick, "as there are evidently some here who are not of an obliging disposition, and as the principle of willing service lies at the root of all social felicity, I would further suggest that, until our Queen is crowned and the Government fairly set up, all such labour shall be undertaken entirely by volunteers."

This proposal was agreed to with boisterous acclaim, and nearly the whole community volunteered on the spot. While this little difficulty was being overcome, Pauline lay sleeping in the palace hard by, and the enthusiastic cheer with which the conclusion of Dominick's speech was received awoke her.

"There—I know'd they'd do it!" exclaimed the lady of the bedchamber fiercely; "lie still, cushla! an' shut your purty eyes. Maybe you'll drop off again!"

A humorous smile beamed in Pauline's countenance and twinkled in her eyes.

"Thank you, dear nurse, I've had enough of sleep. Indeed, I begin to feel so strong that I think I shall very soon be able to undergo that—"

Pauline stopped and burst into a fit of merry laughter.

"It's that caronation, now, ye'll be thinkin' av?" said the widow Lynch, with a reproving look. "Faix, it's no laughin' matter ye'll find it, dear. It's onaisy is the hid as wears a crown."

"Why you talk, nurse, as if you had worn one yourself, and knew all about its troubles."

"Sure, av I didn't, me progenissors did, in Munster, before you English konkered us an' turned us topsy-turvy. But nivver mind. I don't bear no ill-will to 'ee, darlint, bekaise o' the evil deeds o' yer forefathers. I'm of a forgivin' disposition. An' it's a good quane you'll make, too, av ye don't let the men have too much o' their own way. But I do think that you an' me togither'll be more than a match for them all. D'ee think ye could stand the caronation now, dear?"

"Yes, I think I could. But really, you know, I find it so hard to believe it is not all a joke, despite the grave deputations that have waited on me, and the serious arguments they have used. The idea of making me—*Me*—a Queen!"

Again Pauline Rigonda gave way to merry laughter, and again did her lady of the bedchamber administer a reproof by expressing the hope that she might take the matter as lightly a year hence.

This pertinacious reference to possible trouble being mingled with the contemplated honour checked Pauline's disposition to laugh, and she had quite recovered her gravity when her brother Otto entered.

"Pina, I've come to tell you that they've fixed the coronation for Monday next if you feel up to it, and that the new palace

R. M. Ballantyne

is begun—a very different one, let me tell you, from this wretched affair with its tumble-down walls and low roof."

"Indeed—is it so very grand?"

"Grand! I should think it is. Why, it has got three rooms— *three* rooms—think o' that! Not countin' a splendid out-house stuck on behind, about ten feet square and over six feet high. Each of the three rooms is twelve feet long by ten broad; seven feet high, and papered with palm leaves. The middle one is the hall of Audience and Justice—or injustice if you like—the Council Chamber, the House of Parliament, the mess-room, and the drawing-room. The one on the right with two windows, from which are magnificent views, is your Majesty's sleeping-room and boudoir; that on the left is the ditto of Prime Minister Dominick and his Chief Secretary Prince Otto. The sort of hen-coop stuck on behind is to be the abode of the Court Physician, Dr John Marsh—whom, by the way, you'll have to knight—and with whom is to be billeted the Court Jester, Man-at-Arms, Man-of-all-work and general retainer, little Buxley. So, you see, it's all cut and dry, though of course it will take some little time to finish the palace in all its multitudinous details. Meanwhile I have been sent to sound you as to Monday next. Will you be able and ready?"

"If I could only get myself to believe," answered Pauline, as she leaned on one elbow on her couch, and toyed contemplatively with a fold of the shawl that covered her, "that the people are really in earnest, I—"

"Really in earnest!" repeated Otto. "Why, Pina, never were people more in earnest in this world. If you'd heard and seen them talking about it as I have, you'd not doubt their earnestness. Besides, you have no idea how needful you are to the community. The fact is, it is composed of such rough and rowdy elements—though of course there are some respectable and well-principled fellows among them—that nothing short of a power standing high above them and out o' their reach will have any influence with them at all. There are so many strong, determined, and self-willed men amongst them that there's no chance of their ever agreeing to submit to each other; so, you see, you are a sort of good angel, before whom they will be only too glad to bow—a kind of superior being, whom they will reverence, and to whom they will submit—a human safety-valve, in short, to prevent the community from blowing up—a species of—of—"

Here Pauline burst into another of her irrepressible fits of laughter, and being joined therein by Prince Otto, called forth a remonstrance from Mrs Lynch, who declared that if that was the way they were goin' to manage the affairs of state, she would be obliged to advise the settlers to change their minds and set up a republic.

"An' sure, mother," said Otto, who was a privileged favourite, "nothing could be better, with yourself as President."

"Go along wid ye, boy, an' do yer dooty. Tell the people that Miss Pauline will be ready—wind an' weather permittin'."

"Am I to take back that message, Pina?" asked Otto, with a look of glee.

"Well, I suppose you may."

It was not in the nature of things that a coronation in the circumstances which we have described should take place without being more or less intermingled with the unavoidable absurdities which mark the coronations of older and more densely peopled lands. It was felt that as the act was a seriously meant reality, and no mere joke, it should be gone about and accomplished with all due solemnity and proper ceremonial, somewhat after the pattern—as Teddy Malone suggested—of a Lord Mayor's Show; a suggestion, by the way, which did not conduce to the solemnity of the preliminary discussions.

There was one great difficulty, however, with which the embryo nation had to contend, and this was that not one of the community had ever seen a coronation, or knew how the details of the matter should be arranged.

In these circumstances an assembly of the entire nation was convened to consider the matter. As this convention embraced the women (except, of course, the queen elect), it included the babies, and as most of these were self-assertive and well-developed in chest and throat, it was found necessary to relegate them and the women to an outer circle, while the men in an inner circle tackled the problem.

The widow Lynch, being quite irrepressible except by physical force, and even by that with difficulty, was admitted on sufferance to the inner circle, and took part in the discussions.

Like most large assemblies, this one was found so unmanageable, that, after an hour or two of hopeless wrangling, Buxley the tailor started up with dishevelled hair and glaring eyeballs, and uttered a yell that produced a momentary silence. Seizing the moment, he said—

"I moves that we apint a committee to inquire into the whole matter an' report."

"Hear, hear, and well said!" shouted a multitude of voices.

"An' *I* moves," cried Mrs Lynch, starting forward with both arms up and all her fingers rampant, "that—"

"No, no, mother," interrupted Buxley, "you must second the motion."

"Howld yer tongue, ye dirty spalpeen! Isn't it the second motion that I'm puttin'? *I* moves that the committee is Mr Dumnik Rig Gundy an' Dr Marsh—"

"An' *Mister* Nobbs," shouted a voice.

"An' *Mister* Joe Binney," said another.

"An' *little* Mister Buxley, be way of variashun," cried Teddy Malone.

"An' Mistress Lynch, for a change," growled Jabez Jenkins.

"Hear, hear! No, no! Hurrah! Nonsense! Howld yer tongue! Be serious!"—gradually drowned in a confusion of tongues with a yelling accompaniment from infantry in the outer circle.

It was finally agreed, however, that the arrangements for the coronation should be left entirely to a committee composed of Dominick, Dr Marsh, Joe Binney, and Hugh Morris—Joe being put forward as representing the agricultural interest, and Hugh the malcontents. Teddy Malone was added to make an odd number, "for there's luck in odd numbers," as he himself remarked on accepting office.

Immediately after the general meeting broke up, these five retired to the privacy of a neighbouring palm grove, where, seated on a verdant and flowering bank, they proceeded calmly to discuss details.

"You see, my friends," said Dominick, "it must be our most earnest endeavour to carry out this important matter in a serious and business-like manner. Already there is too much of a spirit of levity among the people, who seem to look at the whole affair as a sort of game or joke, playing, as it were, at national life, whereas we actually *are* an independent nation—"

"A small wan, av coorse," murmured Malone.

"Yes, a small one, but not the less real on that account, so that we are entitled to manage our own affairs, arrange our own government, and, generally, to act according to our united will. These islands and their surroundings are unknown—at least they are not put down on any chart; I believe we have discovered them. There are no inhabitants to set up a counter claim; therefore, being entitled to act according to our will, our appointment of a queen to rule us—under limited powers, to be hereafter well considered and clearly written down—is a reality; not a mere play or semi-jest to be undone lightly when the fancy takes us. That being so, we must go to work with gravity and earnestness of purpose."

Teddy Malone, who was an impressionable creature, here became so solemnised that his lengthening visage and seriously wrinkled brow rendered gravity—especially on the part of Dr Marsh—almost impossible.

Overcoming his feelings with a powerful effort the doctor assented to what Dominick said, and suggested that some mild sort of ceremonial should be devised for the coronation, in order to impress the beholders as well as to mark the event.

"That's so," said Teddy Malone, "somethin' quiet an' orderly, like an Irish wake, or—. Ah! then ye needn't smile, doctor. It's the quietest an' most comfortin' thing in life is an Irish wake whin it's gone about properly."

"But we don't want comforting, Teddy," said Dominick, "it is rather a subject for rejoicing."

"Well, then, what's to hinder us rejoicin' in comfort?" returned Teddy. "At all the wakes I ivver attinded there was more rejoicin' than comfortin' goin' on; but that's a matter of taste, av coorse."

"There'll have to be a crown o' some sort," remarked Hugh Morris.

"You're right, lad," said Joe Binney. "It wouldn't do to make it o' pasteboard, would it? P'r'aps that 'ud be too like playin' at a game, an' tin would be little better."

"What else can we make it of, boys?" said Malone, "we've got no goold here—worse luck! but maybe the carpenter cud make wan o' wood. With a lick o' yellow paint it would look genuine."

"Nonsense, Teddy," said the doctor, "don't you see that in this life men should always be guided by circumstances, and act with propriety. Here we are on an island surrounded by coral reefs, going to elect a queen; what more appropriate than that her crown should be made of coral."

"The very thing, doctor," cried Malone, with emphasis, "och! it's the genius ye have! There's all kinds o' coral, red and white, an' we could mix it up wi' some o' that fine-coloured seaweed to make it purty."

"It could be made pritty enough without seaweed," said

Binney, "an' it's my notion that the women-folk would be best at makin' of it."

"Right, Joe, right, so, if you have no objection, we will leave it to them," said Dominick, "and now as to the ceremonial?"

"A pursession," suggested Joe Binney.

"Just so," said Hugh Morris, "the very thing as was in my mind."

"And a throne," cried Malone, "there couldn't be a proper quane widout a throne, you know. The carpenter can make that, anyhow, for there's wood galore on the island—red, black, an' white. Yis, we must have a grand throne, cut, an' carved, an' mounted high, so as she'll have two or three steps to climb up to it."

In regard to the procession and the throne there was considerable difference of opinion, but difficulties were got over and smoothed down at last by the tact and urbanity of Dominick, to whom, finally, the whole question of the coronation was committed. Thus it frequently happens among men. In the multitude of counsellors there is wisdom enough, usually, to guide in the selection of the fittest man to take the helm in all important affairs.

And that reminds us that it is high time to terminate this long digression, and guide our readers back to the beginning of the chapter, where we stated that the important day had at last arrived.

Happily, in those highly favoured climes weather has not usually to be taken much into account. The sun arose out of the ocean's breast with the same unclouded beauty that had marked his rise every morning for a week previously, and would probably mark it for a week to come. The sweet scents of the wooded heights floated down on the silver strand; the sharks ruffled the surface of the lagoon with their black fins, the birds hopped or flew from palm-tree to mimosa-bush, and the waterfowl went about according to taste on lazy or whistling wings, intent on daily business, much as though nothing unusual were "in the air."

But it was otherwise with the human family on Big Island. Unwonted excitement was visible on almost every face. Bustle was in every action. Preparations were going on all round, and, as some members of the community were bent on giving other members a surprise, there was more or less of secrecy and consequent mystery in the behaviour of every one.

By breakfast-time little Mrs Nobbs, the blacksmith's laughter-loving wife, had nearly laughed herself into fits of delight at the crown, which she assisted Mrs Welsh and the widow Lynch to fabricate. The last had devised it, Mrs Welsh had built it in the rough, and Mrs Nobbs had finished it off with the pretty little wreath of red and white branching coral that formed its apex. Apart from taste it was a stupendous erection.

"But don't you think that it's too big and heavy?" cried Mrs Nobbs, with a shrieking giggle and clapping of her hands, as she ran back to have a distant view of it.

"Pooh!" exclaimed Mrs Lynch contemptuously, "too heavy? No, it's nothin', my dear, to what the kings an' quanes of Munster wore."

"But Miss Pauline is neither a king nor a queen of Munster, an' I do think it's a bit over-heavy," objected Mrs Welsh, as she lifted the structure with difficulty.

R. M. Ballantyne

"Well, ye might take off the wreath," was the widow's reply.

Mrs Nobbs removed the only part of the erection that was really pretty, but still it was pronounced by Mrs Welsh to be too heavy, especially for the fair and delicate brows of Pauline Rigonda.

While they were thus engaged Dr Marsh entered the hut, where, for the sake of secrecy, the crown had been prepared, but Dr Marsh was a privileged man, besides he was there professionally; little Brown-eyes was sick—not seriously, but sufficiently so to warrant medical intervention.

"Well, what have we here, ladies?" said the doctor blandly, "part of the throne, eh?"

"Sure it is, in a sort of way, for it's the crown," answered Mrs Lynch, "an' they think it's over-heavy."

"Not at all; by no means," cried the doctor heartily. "It's splendid. Put the wreath on—so. Nothing could be finer. Shall I carry it up for you? The coronation is fixed for noon, you know, so that we may have time to finish off with a grand feast."

"No, no, doctor dear. Thank 'ee kindly, but we must cover it up, so's not to let the people see it till the right time."

"Well, see that you're not late with it."

Having caused Brown-eyes to put out her little tongue, and felt her pulse, and nodded his head gravely once or twice without speaking, all of which must have been highly comforting and beneficial to the child, the doctor went out.

Not long afterwards the people began to assemble round the

palace, in front of which a wondrous throne had been erected. Down in a dell behind a cliff some fifty men had assembled secretly with the crown on a cushion in their midst. They were headed by Dr Marsh, who had been unanimously elected to place the crown on Pauline's head. In the palace Pauline was being prepared by Mrs Lynch and Mrs Nobbs for the ceremony.

On the top of a mound close to the palace a band of conspirators was assembled. These conspirators were screened from view by some thick bushes. Otto Rigonda was their ringleader, Teddy Malone and little Buxley formed the rest of the band. Otto had found a dead tree. Its trunk had been hollowed by decay. He and his fellow-conspirators had sawn it off near to the ground, and close to the root they had drilled a touch-hole. This huge piece of ordnance they had loaded with a heavy charge of the ship's gunpowder. Otto now stood ready with a piece of slow-match at the touch-hole, and another piece, lighted, in hand.

Suddenly, about the hour of noon, Abel Welsh the carpenter, and Nobbs the blacksmith, issued from the palace with two long tin implements. Secretly, for two weeks previously, had these devoted men retired every night to the opposite extremity of Big Island, and frightened into fits the birds and beasts of that region with the sounds they produced in practising on those instruments. Applying the trumpets to their lips, they sent forth a tremendous, though not uniform, blast.

The surrounding crowd, who expected something, but knew not what, replied with a cheer not unmixed with laughter, for the two trumpets, after the manner of asses, had to make some ineffectual preliminary efforts before achieving a full-toned bray. An answering note from the dell, however, repressed the laughter and awoke curiosity. Next moment the doctor appeared carrying the crown, and followed by his fifty men, armed with muskets, rifles, fowling-pieces, and revolvers. Their appearance was so realistic and impressive that the people forgot to cheer. At the same moment the palace door was thrown open, and Dominick led the youthful queen to the foot of the throne.

Poor little Pauline looked so modest and pretty, and even timid, and withal so angelically innocent in the simplicity of her attire, that the people burst into an earnestly enthusiastic shout, and began for the first time to feel that this was no game or play, but a serious reality.

Things had been so arranged that Pina and Dr Marsh reached the foot of the throne together. Then the latter took the pretty coral wreath off the huge crown, and, to widow Lynch's felt, but not expressed, indignation, placed *that* on Pauline's head.

"Pauline Rigonda," he said in a loud voice, "I have been appointed by the people of this island to crown you, in their name and by their authority, as Queen of Refuge Islands, in the full belief that your innocence and regard for truth and righteousness will be their best guarantee that you will select as your assistants the men whom you think best suited to aid you in the promotion of good government."

The serious tone of the doctor's voice, and the genuine shouts of satisfaction from the people, put the poor little queen in such a flutter that nearly all her courage forsook her, and she could scarcely reply. Nevertheless, she had a mind of her own.

"Doctor Marsh, and my dear people," she said at last, "I—I scarcely know how to reply. You overrate me altogether; but—but, if I rule at all, I will do so by the blessed truths of this book (she held up a Bible); and—and before taking a single step further I appoint as my—my Prime Minister—if I may so call him—Joe Binney."

For one moment there was the silence of amazement, for neither Dominick nor Dr Marsh knew of Pauline's intention. Only the widow Lynch had been aware of her resolve. Next moment a hilarious cheer burst from the crowd, and Teddy Malone, from his retreat, shouted, "God bliss the Quane!" which infused hearty laughter into the cheer, whereupon Welsh and Nobbs, thinking the right time had come, sent out of their tin tubes, after a few ineffectual blurts, two terrific brays. Fearing to be too late, one of the armed men let off his piece, which was the signal for a grand *feu de joie*.

"Now for it," thought the chief conspirator in the bushes, as he applied his light to the slow-match. He thought nothing more just then, for the slow-match proved to be rather quick, fired the powder at once, and the monster cannon, bursting with a hideous roar into a thousand pieces, blew Otto through the bushes and down the mound, at the foot of which he lay as one dead.

Consternation was on every face. The queen, dropping her crown, sprang to his side, Dr Marsh did the same, but Otto recovered almost immediately.

"That *was* a stunner!" he said, with a confused look, putting his hand to his head, as they helped him to rise.

Strange to say, he was none the worse of the misadventure, but did his part nobly at the Royal feast that followed.

That night she who had risen with the sun as Pauline Rigonda, laid her fair young head upon the pillow as—the Island Queen.

CHAPTER NINE

SHOWS HOW THEY WERE TORMENTED BY AN OLD FAMILIAR FIEND; HOW THEY KILLED HIM, AND WHAT BEFELL THE QUEEN AND OTTO WHILE IN THE PURSUIT OF LEGITIMATE PLEASURE

When the widow Lynch told Pauline that "onaisy is the hid as wears a crown," she stated a great truth which was borne in upon the poor queen at the very commencement of her reign.

Up to that time Malines had quietly kept possession of the key of the ship's liquor-room, knowing full well what extreme danger lay in letting men have unrestrained command of strong drink. But when the royal feast referred to in the last chapter was pending, he could not well refuse to issue an allowance of grog. He did so, however, on the understanding that only a small quantity was to be taken for the occasion, and that he should himself open and lock the door for them. He made this stipulation because he knew well enough the men who wanted to drink would break the door open if he refused to give up the key; and his fears were justified, for some of the more mutinous among the men, under the leadership of Jabez Jenkins and Morris, seized the key from the mate when he produced it, carried all the spirit and wine casks to the shore, ferried them over the lagoon to Big Island, and set them up ostentatiously and conspicuously in a row not far from the palace. As this was understood by the people to be in connection with the coronation festivities, no particular notice was taken of it.

But the result soon began to be felt, for after the festivities were over, and most of the settlers had retired to rest, a group of kindred souls gathered round the spirit casks, and went in for what one of them termed a "regular spree." At first they drank and chatted with moderate noise, but as the fumes of the terrible fire-water mounted to their brains they began to shout and sing, then to quarrel and fight, and, finally, the wonted silence of the night was wildly disturbed by the oaths and fiendish yells and idiotic laughter of maniacs.

"This won't do," said Dominick, issuing from his room in the palace, and meeting the doctor.

"I had just come to the same conclusion," said the latter, "and was about to consult you as to what we should do."

"Collect some of our best men and put a stop to it," returned Dominick; "but here comes the prime minister—roused, no doubt, as we have been. What say you, Joe; shall we attempt to quell them?"

"Well, master, that depends. There's a braw lot on 'em, an' if they beant far gone, d'ee see, they might gie us a deal o' trouble. If they *be* far gone I'd advise ye to let 'em alone; the drink'll quell 'em soon enough. Arter that we'll know what to do."

Just as he spoke a woman was seen rushing frantically towards them. It was little Mrs Nobbs. Poor thing! All her wonted merriment had fled from her comely face, and been supplanted by a look of horror.

"O sirs!" she cried, clasping her hands, and gasping as she spoke, "come, come quick, my John has falled an' broke his pledge, an' he's goin' to murder some of 'em. I *know* he'll do it; he's got hold o' the fore-hammer. Oh! come quick!"

They required no urging. Running down to the scene of the orgies, they found that the blacksmith, who had hitherto been considered—and really was—one of the quietest men of the party, was now among the drunkards. He stood in the midst of the rioters, his large frame swaying to and fro, while he held the ponderous fore-hammer threateningly in his hands, and insanity gleamed in his eyes as he glared fiercely at Jabez Jenkins.

On Jabez the liquor had a different effect, his temperament being totally different. He was a rather phlegmatic man, and, having drunk enough to have driven two men like the blacksmith raving mad, he only stood before him with a dull heavy look of stupidity, mingled with an idiotic sneer of defiance.

"Fiend!" shouted Nobbs, gnashing his teeth, "you have got me to do it, and now I'll smash in your thick skull—I'll—"

He stopped abruptly for a moment. Joe Binney came up behind and gently laid a hand on his shoulder.

"Come, John, you ain't agoin' to do it. You knows you're not."

The quiet tone, the gentle yet fearless look, and, above all, the sensible, kindly expression on his friend's countenance, effectually subdued the blacksmith for a few seconds, but the fury soon returned, though the channel in which it flowed was changed, for Jabez was forgotten, having slunk away.

"Ha!" he shouted, grasping Joe by the hand and arm, "I've had it again! You don't know how it shoots through my veins. I—I've tried to break with it, too—tried—tried! D'ee know what it is to try, Joe, to try—try—try till your blood curdles, an' your marrow boils, and your nerves tingle—but I gained the victory once—I—ha! ha! yes, I took the pledge an' kep' it, an' I've bin all right—till to-night. My Mary knows that. She'll tell you it's true—for months, and months, and months, and—but I'll keep it *yet*!"

He shouted his last words in a tone of fierce defiance, let go his friend, caught up the sledge-hammer, and, whirling it round his head as if it had been a mere toy, turned to rush towards the sea.

But Joe's strong arm arrested him. Well did he understand the nature of the awful fiend, with which the blacksmith was fighting. The scene enacting was, with modifications, somewhat familiar to him, for he had dwelt near a great city where many a comrade had fallen in the same fight, never more to rise in this life.

Joe's superior strength told for a moment, and he held the struggling madman fast, but before Dominick and the doctor could spring to his aid, Nobbs had burst from him. The brief check, however, seemed to have changed his intentions. Possibly he was affected by some hazy notion that it would be a quicker end to leap headlong from the neighbouring cliffs than to plunge into the sea. At all events, he ran like a deer up towards the woods. A bonfire, round which the revellers had made merry, lay in his path. He went straight through it, scattering the firebrands right and left. No one attempted, no one dared, to stop him, but God put a check in his way. The course he had taken brought him straight up to the row of casks which stood on the other side of the fire, and again his wild mood was changed. With a yell of triumph he brought the sledge-hammer down on one of the casks, drove in the head, and overturned it with the same blow, and the liquor gushing out flowed into the fire, where it went up in a magnificent roar of flame.

The effect on those of the rioters who were not too drunk to understand anything, was to draw forth a series of wild cheers, but high above these rang the triumphant shout of the blacksmith as he gazed at the destruction of his enemy.

By this time all the people in the settlement had turned out, and were looking on in excitement, alarm, or horror, according to temperament. Among them, of course, was the widow Lynch, who was quick to note that events were taking a favourable turn. Springing boldly to the side of the smith, and, in her wild dishevelment of hair and attire, seeming a not unfit companion, she cried—

"Don't spare them, John! sure there's another inimy close at yer back."

Nobbs had sense enough left to observe something of the ludicrous in the woman and her advice. He turned at once, uttered a wildly jovial laugh, and driving in the head of another cask, overturned it. As before, the spirit rushed down the hill and was set ablaze, but the poor madman did not pause now to look at the result. His great enemy was in his power; his spirit was roused. Like one of the fabled heroes of old, he laid about him with his ponderous weapon right and left until every cask was smashed, and every drop of the accursed liquid was rushing down the hillside to the sea, or flaming out its fierce existence in the air.

The people looked on awe-stricken, and in silence, while the madman fought. It was not with the senseless casks or the inanimate liquor that poor John Nobbs waged war that night;

it was with a real fiend who, in days gone by, had many a time tripped him up and laid him low, who had nearly crushed the heart of his naturally cheerful little wife, who had ruined his business, broken up his home, alienated his friends, and, finally, driven him into exile—a fiend from whom, for many months, under the influence of "the pledge," he had been free, and who, he had fondly hoped, was quite dead.

This sudden revival of the old foe, and this unexpected surprise and fall, had roused this strong man's spirit to its utmost ferocity, and in mighty wrath he plied his hammer like a second Thor. But the very strength and nervous power of the man constituted his weakness, when brought under the subtle influence of the old tempter, and it is probable that on his recovery, with nerves shaken, old cravings awakened, and self-respect gone, he would have fallen again and again if God had not made use of the paroxysm of rage to destroy the opportunity and the cause of evil. Nobbs did not know at that time, though he learned it afterwards, that safety from the drink-sin—as from all other sin—lies not in strong-man resolutions, or Temperance pledges, though both are useful aids, but in Jesus, the Saviour *from sin*.

Some of those who witnessed the wholesale destruction of the liquor would fain have made an effort to prevent it; but, fortunately for the community, most of them were too drunk to care, and the others to interfere; while all were so taken by surprise that the deed was done and the grand conflagration ended before they had realised the full significance of the blacksmith's act.

When the last head had been driven in, and the last gallon of spirit summarily dismissed by the fire, Nobbs threw up his arms, and, looking upward, gave vent to a cheer which ended in a prolonged cry. For a moment he stood thus, then the hammer dropt from his grasp, and he fell back insensible.

Poor little Mrs Nobbs was by his side on her knees in a moment, parting the dark hair from his broad brow, kissing his swart cheeks, and chafing his strong hands.

"O John! darling John!" she cried, "come back—come back—don't die. You never was hard or cruel to *me*! Even the drink could not do that. Come back, John!"

Dr Marsh here gently restrained her. "Don't be alarmed," he said, as he undid the smith's necktie; "he'll be all right presently. Stand back, don't crowd round him; and you go fetch a cup of water, Mrs Nobbs."

The reassuring tones and the necessity for action did much to calm the excited woman. Before she had returned with the water her husband had partially recovered. They carried him to his hut, and left him to sleep off the effects, while his poor little wife watched by his side. When left quite alone, she went down on her knees beside him, and prayed for his deliverance with all her heart. Then she rose and sat down with a calm, contented look, muttering, "Yes; He *is* the hearer and answerer of prayer. He *will* answer me."

She might have gone further and said, "He *has* answered me," for was not the destruction of the liquor an answer to the petition before it was put up? "Before they call I will answer."

"Pina," said Otto the following day, in a tone almost of reproach, during a private audience with the queen, "Pina, how came you to do such an insane thing as choose Joe Binney for your premier? Why didn't you choose Dom? You know well enough that he's fifty times cleverer than Joe, and even in the matter of strength, though he's not so strong, I'm very sure that with his pugilistic powers he could keep order quite as well. Besides, all the people had made up their minds, as a matter of course, that Dom was to be premier, and then—he's a gentleman."

"I'm thankful that you are not one of the Privy Council, Otto," returned Pauline, with a laugh. "You put several questions, and a string of commentary and suggestion in the same breath! Let me answer you in detail, beginning with your last remark. Joe is a gentleman in the highest sense of that word. He is gentle as a lamb by nature, and a *man* every inch of him. But, more than this, I have noticed that he is a peculiarly wise man, with a calm, pool head on all occasions, and not too ready to use his great physical power in the settlement of disputes. I have observed, too, that when asked for his advice, he usually thinks well before he gives it, and when his advice is followed things almost always go well. Still further, Joe has the thorough confidence of the people, and I am not so sure that Dom has. Besides, if I had appointed Dom, some of the ungenerous among them might have said it was done from mere favouritism. Then as to the people making up their minds that I would appoint Dom," continued Pauline, "what have I to do with *that*?"

"Why, everything to do with it," returned Otto, with a surprised look. "Were you not made queen for the purpose of carrying out their wishes?"

"Certainly not," answered Pauline; "I was made queen for the purpose of ruling. They told me they had confidence in my judgment, not in my readiness to carry out their wishes. If my judgment, coupled with that of my advisers, does not suit them, it is open to them to unmake me as they made me, and appoint a king or a president, but my judgment I cannot alter."

R. M. Ballantyne

Otto listened to these gravely stated opinions of the new queen with increasing astonishment.

"Then, you awful despot," he said, "do you mean to tell me that you are going to have no regard for the will of the people?"

"No, I don't mean to tell you that, you presumptuous little subject. I intend always to have the utmost regard for the will of my people, and to weigh it well, and consult with my advisers about it; and when our united judgment says that their will is good, I will act in accordance with it; when we think it bad, I will reject it. I have been made queen to rule, and I *mean* to rule! That's fair, isn't it? If they don't like my ruling they can dethrone me. That's also fair, isn't it? You wouldn't have me become a mere puppet—a jumping Jack or Jinnie—would you, for the people to pull the string of?"

"Well, I never!" exclaimed Otto, gazing with distended eyes at the soft fair face and at the pretty little innocent mouth that gave vent to these vigorous sentiments. "And what may it be your majesty's pleasure to do next?"

"It is my pleasure that you, sir, shall go down to the beach and prepare the dinghy for immediate service. I have already directed the prime minister, in conjunction with Dom and our Court physician, to draw up a constitution and code of laws; while they are thus employed you and I will go a-fishing."

"Very good; I suppose I'm bound to obey, but I thought your majesty preferred to go a-sketching."

"We will do both. Be off, sirrah!"

Otto was not long in launching and getting ready the little

punt, or dinghy, belonging to the wreck, which, being too small for carrying goods to the island, had been made over to Pauline as a royal barge for her special amusement, and already had she and her little brother enjoyed several charming expeditions among the sheltered islets of the lagoon, when Otto devoted himself chiefly to rowing and fishing, while his sister sketched with pencil and water-colours. Being expert with both, she took great pleasure therein.

"It *is* so pleasant and so very engrossing," she murmured, busying herself with a sketch of Otto as he rowed gently towards one of the smaller islets. "I can't tell you how much I delight—turn your head a little more to the left—so—and do keep your nose quiet if you can."

"Impossible," said Otto. "There's a little fly that has made up its mind to go into my nose. I can neither drive it away nor catch it while both hands are engaged with the oars, so there's no resource left but to screw my nose about. But what were you going to say you delighted in?"

"In—in drawing," replied the queen very slowly, while her pretty little head went up and down as she glanced alternately at her sitter and the sketch-book on her knee; "it—it takes one's mind—so—off—"

"The cares of state?" said Otto. "Yes, I can easily understand what a-re-re-ha! hk-sh!" he gave way to a convulsive sneeze; "there, it went up at last, and that little fly's doom is sealed!"

"I should think it was," said Pauline laughingly. "To be blown from a cannon's mouth must be nothing to that. Now, do keep still, just for one minute."

For considerably more than a minute she went on sketching busily, while her brother pulled along very gently, as if unwilling to break the pleasant silence. Everything around was calculated to foster a dreamy, languid, peaceful state of mind. The weather was pleasantly cool—just cool enough to render the brilliant sunshine most enjoyable. Not a zephyr disturbed the glassy surface of the sea outside or the lagoon within, or broke the perfect reflections of the islets among which they moved. The silence would have been even oppressive had it not been for the soft, plaintive cries of wildfowl and the occasional whistling of wings as they hurried to and fro, and the solemn boom of the great breakers as they fell at slow regular intervals on the reef. "Doesn't it sound," said Pauline, looking up from her sketch with a flush of delight, "like the deep soft voice of the ocean speaking peace to all mankind?"

"What, the breakers?" asked Otto.

"Yes, dropping with a soft deep roar as they do in the midst of the universal silence."

"Well, it doesn't quite strike me in that light, Pina. My imagination isn't so lively as yours. Seems to me more like the snoring of a sleeping giant, whom it is best to let lie still like a sleeping dog, for he's apt to do considerable damage when roused."

The soft influences around soon reduced the pair to silence again. After a time it was broken by Pauline.

"What are you thinking of, Otto?"

"I was thinking, your majesty, that it seems unfair, after making Joe prime minister, Dom a privy councillor, the doctor Court physician and general humbug, that you should give me no definite position in the royal household."

"What would you say to being commander of the forces?" asked Pauline dreamily, as she put in a few finishing touches, "for then, you see, you might adopt the title which you have unfairly bestowed on the doctor—General Humbug."

Otto shook his head. "Wouldn't do, my dear queen. Not being a correct description, your bestowing it would compromise your majesty's well-known character for truthfulness. What d'you say to make me a page—page in waiting?"

"You'll have to turn over a new leaf if I do, for a page is supposed to be quiet, respectful, polite, obedient, ready—"

"No use to go further, Pina. I'm not cut out for a page. Will you land on this islet?"

They were gliding softly past one of the most picturesque and verdant gems of the lagoon at the time.

"No, I've taken a fancy to make a sketch from that one nearer to the shore of Big Island. You see, there is not only a very picturesque group of trees on it just at that place, but the background happens to be filled up by a distant view of the prettiest part of our settlement, where Joe Binney's garden lies, close to Mrs Lynch's garden, with its wonderfully shaped and curious hut, (no wonder, built by herself!) and a corner of the palace rising just behind the new schoolhouse."

"Mind your eye, queen, else you go souse overboard when we strike," said Otto, not without reason, for next moment the dinghy's keel grated on the sand of the islet, and Pauline, having risen in her eagerness to go to work, almost fulfilled the boy's prediction.

"But tell me, Pina, what do you mean to do with that schoolhouse when it is built?" asked Otto, as he walked beside his sister to the picturesque spot above referred to.

"To teach in it, of course."

"What—yourself?"

"Well, yes, to some extent. Of course I cannot do much in that way—"

"I understand—the affairs of state!" said Otto, "will not permit, etcetera."

"Put it so if you please," returned Pauline, laughing. "Here, sit down; help me to arrange my things, and I'll explain. You cannot fail to have been impressed with the fact that the children of the settlers are dreadfully ignorant."

"H'm! I suppose you are right; but I have been more deeply impressed with the fact that they are dreadfully dirty, and desperately quarrelsome, and deplorably mischievous."

"Just so," resumed Pauline. "Now, I intend to get your friend Redding, who was once a schoolmaster, to take these children in hand when the schoolroom is finished, and teach them what he can, superintended by Dr Marsh, who volunteered his services the moment I mentioned the school. In the evenings I will take the mothers in hand, and teach them their duties to their children and the community—"

"Being yourself such an old and experienced mother," said Otto.

"Silence, sir! you ought to remember that we have a dear, darling mother at home, whose character is engraven on my memory, and whom I can hold up as a model."

"True, Pina! The dear old mother!" returned Otto, a burst of home-feeling interfering for a moment with his levity. "Just you paint her portrait fair and true, and if they come anything within a hundred miles o' the mark yours will be a kingd—queendom, I mean—of amazin' mothers. I sometimes fear," continued the boy, becoming grave, "it may be a long time before we set eyes on mother again."

"I used to fear the same," said Pauline, "but I have become more hopeful on that point since Dr Marsh said he was determined to have a small schooner built out of the wreck, and attempt with a few sailors to reach England in her, and report our condition here."

"Why, that would do you out of your kingdom, Pina!"

"It does not follow. And what if it did?"

"It would be a pity. Not pleasant you know, to be dethroned. But to return to mother. D'you think the old cat will have learned to speak by this time?"

To this Pauline replied that she feared not; that, although the cat might have mastered the consonants, it could never have managed the vowels. "Dear mother," she added, in a more earnest tone, "I am quite sure that though the cat may not speak to her, she will not have ceased to speak to the cat. Now, go away, Otto, you're beginning to make me talk nonsense."

"But what about the schoolhouse?" persisted the boy, while the girl began to sketch the view. "You have not finished that subject."

"True—well, besides teaching the mothers I have great hopes of inducing Dom to set up a Sunday-school, in which those

R. M. Ballantyne

who feel inclined might be taught out of the Bible, and that might in time lead to our making a church of it on Sundays, and having regular services, for there are some earnest Christians among the men, who I feel quite sure would be ready to help in the work. Then as to an army—"

"An army!" echoed Otto, "what do we want with an army? who have we to fight against?"

Little did Otto or Pauline think that at the very time they were conversing thus pleasantly on that beautiful islet, the presence of a friendly army was urgently required, for there in the bushes close behind them listening to every sentence, but understanding never a word, lay a group of tattooed and armed savages!

In the prosecution of evil designs, the nature of which was best known to themselves, these savages had arrived at Refuge Islands the night before. Instantly they became aware of the presence of the white men, and took measures to observe them closely without being themselves observed. Carrying their war-canoe over the reef in the dark, and launching it on the lagoon, they advanced as near to the settlement as possible, landed a small party on an islet, and then retired with the canoe. It was this party which lay in ambush so near to our little hero and heroine. They had been watching the settlers since daybreak, and were not a little surprised, as well as gratified, by the unexpected arrival of the little boat.

The savage who lay there grinning like a Cheshire cat, and peeping through the long grass not ten feet from where the brother and sister sat, was a huge man, tattooed all over, so that his face resembled carved mahogany, his most prominent feature being a great flat nose, with a blue spot on the point of it.

Suddenly Otto caught sight of the glitter of this man's eyes and teeth.

Now, the power of self-restraint was a prominent feature in Otto's character, at least in circumstances of danger, though in the matter of fun and mischief he was rather weak. No sign did Otto give of his discovery, although his heart seemed to jump into his mouth. He did not even check or alter the tone of his conversation, but he changed the subject with surprising abruptness. He had brought up one of the dinghy's oars on his shoulder as a sort of plaything or vaulting-pole. Suddenly, asking Pauline if she had ever seen him balance an oar on his chin, he proceeded to perform the feat, much to her amusement. In doing so he turned his back completely on the savage in ambush, whose cattish grin increased as the boy staggered about.

But there was purpose in Otto's staggering. He gradually lessened the distance between himself and the savage. When near enough for his purpose, he grasped the oar with both hands, wheeled sharply round, and brought the heavy handle of it down with such a whack on the bridge of the savage's blue-spotted nose that he suddenly ceased to grin, and dropped his proboscis in the dust!

At the same instant, to the horror and surprise of the brother and sister, up sprang half a dozen hideous natives, who seized them, placed their black hands on their mouths, and bore them swiftly away. The war-canoe, putting off from its concealment, received the party along with the fallen leader, and made for the reef.

High on the cliffs of Big Island Dr John Marsh had been smilingly watching the proceedings of the queen and her brother in the dinghy. When he witnessed the last act of the play, however, the smile vanished. With a bound that would have done credit to a kangaroo, and a roar that would have shamed a lion, he sprang over the cliffs, ran towards the beach, and was followed—yelling—by all the men at hand—some armed, and some not. They leaped into the largest boat on the shore, put out the ten oars, bent to them with a will, and skimmed over the lagoon in fierce pursuit.

Soon the savages gained the reef, carried their canoe swiftly over, and launched on the open sea, cutting through the great rollers like a rocket or a fish-torpedo.

Heavy timbers and stout planks could not be treated thus; nevertheless, the white men were so wild and strong, that when the boat finally gained the open sea it was not very far behind the canoe.

CHAPTER TEN

DESCRIBES A RESCUE, A CONSPIRACY, AND A TRIAL

Proverbially a stern chase is a long one. Happily, there are exceptions to proverbs as well as rules. The chase of the war-canoe, however, with the captured queen on board, did not promise to be exceptional at first, for the canoe was light and sharp, and powerfully manned, so that the savages could relieve each other frequently, whereas the settlers' boat was heavy and blunt, and not by any means too full of men. It soon became apparent that the latter was no match for the former under oars. The distance between the two visibly increased.

Dr Marsh steered. He was deadly pale, and there was a peculiarly intense expression of anxiety in the steady gaze, with which he watched the ever-diminishing canoe.

"No chance?" muttered Jabez Jenkins, who happened to form one of the crew and pulled the bow oar.

"No chance?" repeated Dominick, who also pulled one of the oars. "There's *every* chance. We're sure to tire them out. Ho! lads, give way with a will!"

Although labouring already with all his might, indignation at Jenkins's remark enabled him to put on a spurt, which the others imitated. Still the distance between boat and canoe increased.

"They are three to one," growled Malines, who, up to that time, had been doing his best.

"Silence!" thundered the doctor, drawing a revolver from his pocket and cocking it.

Beads of perspiration stood on the doctor's brow, and there was something so terrible in the look of his white face that no one ventured to utter another word, but all pulled as if for their lives.

For some minutes no sound was heard save the regular rattle of the oars in the rowlocks, the swish of the foam as it flew from the cutwater, and the occasional sob or gasp of the men as they exerted themselves to the utmost limit of their powers in the hopeless pursuit.

Suddenly Teddy Malone cried eagerly, "Look out—astern!"

All turned their gaze as directed, and observed a dark line on the horizon.

"Thank God!" murmured the doctor, "a breeze!"

It was indeed true. Just at this critical moment of profound, despair, a gleam of hope was sent to sustain them! Is it not often thus in the dealings of God with man?

There was no relaxation of effort, however, on the part of the crew until the breeze bore down on them. Then the mate and Hugh Morrison, drawing in their oars, set up the mast and hoisted the sails. Instantly the good craft bent over, as if bowing submissively to her rightful lord, and the gurgling water rolled swiftly from her prow. Still the men plied the oars, but now with the strength of hope, until the breeze freshened so much as to render their further use unnecessary.

"Now, indeed, the tables are turned," said Dominick with a great sigh of relief, as he drew in his oar.

"Yes; if the wind holds," said the doctor, glancing back anxiously.

"It'll howld," said Malone firmly.

"Who made you so sure a judge of weather?" demanded Jenkins.

"Sure it isn't me as is judge. It's the widdy. She says to me this mornin', says she, 'The'll be a stiff breeze afore night, Teddy,' an' I nivver found the widdy wrong in her forecasts o' the weather."

"The distance decreases rapidly! Hurrah! boys, we'll catch them yet," cried Dominick.

This was obviously the case. With her large sails filled by a stiff breeze almost directly astern, the boat went through the water like "a thing of life." The savages, perceiving this, redoubled their efforts, but in vain. The pursuers gained on them rapidly.

An exclamation of surprise burst from those in the boat as they observed two splashes, one on either side of the canoe, as if some one had fallen or leaped overboard. A great shout from the savages followed, and they suddenly ceased to paddle. The canoe was still too far off for the pursuers to make out what had occurred; but in another minute they observed that two round black objects emerged from the water some distance astern of the canoe. The savages also saw these, and uttered a frightful yell as they backed their craft towards them.

"They've jumped overboard!" exclaimed Dominick. "Now, boys—ready with your guns!"

No need for this order. All were ready in a second, but none dared to fire for fear of hitting the swimmers.

Just then a savage rose in the stern of the canoe and poised a short spear.

Instantly every gun in the boat was pointed.

"Not a shot!" shouted Dr Marsh, as he sprang forward with a double-barrelled rifle in his hand.

"Keep her away two points!" he cried, as he knelt to take aim. Every one was well aware of the doctor's power of shooting, and waited the result with bated breath. The savage seemed to bend backward for the cast of the spear. At that moment the crack of the doctor's rifle was heard, and the right arm of the savage fell.

Another savage caught up the spear, and urged his comrades, apparently, to back the canoe still further; but they had got a fright, and were evidently unwilling to do so. Before they could make up their minds, another shot from the doctor's rifle sent the second savage headlong into the bottom of the canoe.

"Give them a volley now, lads," he said, turning round and resuming his place at the helm; "but fire high."

The rattling volley which followed, and the whistle of the leaden hail over their heads, quickly settled the savage minds. One of their paddles, which chanced to be held aloft at the moment, was shot into splinters, and precipitated their decision. With a howl of rage and terror they dipped their paddles into the sea and flew ahead.

"Be ready there," cried the doctor, as he anxiously guided the boat.

Teddy Malone, Morris, Dominick, and Jabez leaned eagerly over the bows with outstretched arms and clawlike fingers. Another moment and Queen Pina with Otto were rescued from the deep, as well as from several sharks, which, doubtless, had been licking their lips at the prospect of the royal feast in store for them.

"Ain't you goin' to carry on, an' sink the varmints?" exclaimed Jabez in surprise, as the doctor put the helm hard down, and prepared to return home.

"No," replied the doctor sharply.

During the voyage out the crew of the wrecked ship had become intimately acquainted with the doctor's qualities, among others that there was a certain quiet tone in his "no" which was final. To put the belligerents of the party more at rest, however, Dominick backed his friend up by adding that he had no ill-will to the miserable savages; that they had been punished enough already; that they had got all they wanted from them; and that as their own party consisted chiefly of settlers, not warriors, there was no occasion for fighting.

"Speak for yourself, Dom," cried Otto, as he wrung the water out of his garments. "If I was in that canoe with a good carving-knife, I'd be warrior enough to give a settler to the baboon wi' the swelled nose who crammed me into a—"

The remainder of the speech was drowned in laughter, for Otto spoke with intense indignation, as he thought of the injuries and indignities he had so recently suffered.

"Why, what did they do to you, Otto?" asked his brother.

"Oh! I can't tell you," replied the other; "I'm too mad. Tell 'em, Pina."

Queen Pina, who had also been engaged for some minutes in wringing the water from her skirts, sat down, and, in the sweetest of voices, told how they had been surprised on the islet, how Otto had flattened a chief's nose with an oar, and how they had afterwards been carried off.

"Then," she added, "when they saw that you were unable to overtake them, the chief with the swelled nose began to beat poor Otto and pull his hair savagely. I do believe he would have killed him if a man, who seemed to be the leader of them all, had not ordered him to desist. When you put up the sail and began to overtake us, the chief with the swelled nose got out a rough kind of sack and tried to thrust Otto into it. While he was struggling with this chief—"

"Fighting," interrupted Otto; "fighting with the baboon."

"Well, fighting, if you prefer it—he asked me if I was brave?"

"No, I didn't; I said game."

"Well—if I was game to jump overboard at the same moment that he did? I quickly said yes. He twisted himself out of the man's—"

"Baboon's! baboon's!"

"Well—baboon's grasp, and went over the side like an eel, and—"

"And she," interrupted Otto, "she went plump on the other side like a sack of potatoes, and we met under the canoe and dived well astern before coming up for breath. You know what pains you took with our swimming and diving, Dom; it helped us then, I can tell you; and so here we are, all alive and hearty. But I saw the black fellow goin' to send a spear at Pina, and can't think why he didn't let fly. P'r'aps he did, and missed."

"No, he didn't; for Dr Marsh shot him in the arm," said Dominick, "and thus saved Pauline's life."

"Three cheers for the Queen!" cried little Buxley, who had done good service at the oar, and whose little bosom was filled with enthusiasm at the recital of this adventure.

The invitation was heartily responded to.

"An' wan more for the doctor!" shouted Malone.

In this rejoicing frame of mind they returned to Big Island, where Pauline was received with a warm embrace by the widow Lynch, who had been dancing about the settlement in a more or less deranged state ever since the boat left.

That same evening two meetings of considerable importance took place in the palace. The first was a cabinet council in the hall; the other a meeting of conspirators in the back-kitchen. Both were brief, for each was interrupted. We will take the cabinet council first.

The ministers present at it were the premier, Dominick and Dr Marsh, both of whom Joe had called to his aid.

"Now, my dear queen," said the premier, "we have met to consider the constitution; but before saying a word about it myself, I would like to hear what your majesty has to say about it."

"I'm not sure," said the queen gravely, "that I have the faintest notion as to how a constitution should begin or end. But I will give you a motto to set in the forefront of our constitution, which may also form the foundation on which it is to be built—the pattern to which its parts must conform. It is this: 'Whatsoever ye would that men should do to you, do ye even so to them.'"

"I will set that down with pleasure," said Dominick, who acted as clerk, but, before he could write a line, a knock at the door interrupted them. Then the door opened, and Otto's head appeared with eagerness in the eyes, and a beckoning hand in advance.

Dominick rose and went out.

"I've just overheard Morris and Jabez in the back-kitchen making an appointment. Shall I tell our squad to be ready?"

"Where is the appointed place?" asked Dominick.

"On the reef. They start this very night, for the wind suits, and I heard Hugh say that all was ready."

"Good! I didn't think the game was so nearly played out. Well for us that we are prepared. Yes, call up the squad.

We'll give them checkmate to-night."

It must be explained here that ever since the night of the discovery of the plot organised by Morris to seize and carry off the wrecked ship, Otto and his brother had kept a close watch on the men, and were aware of all their plans and intended movements. They had also communicated their knowledge to a select few, whom Otto styled the squad, who had pledged themselves to be ready at a moment's notice to do their best to circumvent the conspirators. Among other things Otto had discovered that Malines had agreed to join them, professing himself quite willing to act as second in command under Morris.

It may also be explained that though we have hitherto spoken of the vessel which had been cast on the reef as a wreck, it was in reality very slightly injured about the hull, and much of the damage done to the spars and rigging had been quietly repaired by the conspirators.

When darkness shrouded land and sea, two expeditions started from the settlement that night—one following the other. The conspirators in the largest boat set off first. As it was no unusual thing for a night expedition to the reef in order to transport supplies from the wreck in the morning, the departure of the large boat attracted little notice.

When it had got well away a smaller boat set off, containing the "squad," which numbered among its members Dominick, the doctor, Otto, Joe, and his brother David, Teddy Malone, little Buxley, John Nobbs the blacksmith, and others, all of whom were armed with revolvers.

They steered for a different part of the reef, so as to avoid being seen by the conspirators. On landing they passed through the old burial-ground and made for the Golden

Cave. This place had, since the settlement on Big Island, been given over entirely to Pauline's use, and being styled the Queen's seaside palace, no one ever thought of entering it without permission. Hence the party of observation knew that it would be a secure place of ambush.

When safe inside, Dominick and Otto were deputed to go out as quietly as possible, note what Morris and his men were doing, and bring back a report.

"For," said the doctor, "if we interrupt them too soon they may pretend that this is one of their ordinary visits to the ship for supplies, and if we are too late they may get clear away in spite of us. We must strike when the iron is hot."

"Yes," said Otto, looking back as he followed his brother, "we'll look well to the heating process and let you know when they're white hot, so have your revolvers ready, my braves!"

"Och! shut your tatie-trap," cried Malone, but Otto, having shut the door, lost the advice.

The night was neither decidedly light nor dark. There might, indeed, to have been moonlight, but clouds veiled the light though they could not altogether obscure it; thus there was just enough to render objects dimly visible.

"All the better," whispered Dominick, as they turned the point of rock that hid the wreck from view. "We'll go down by the thicket. Keep close to my heels, boy, and drop on your hands and knees when you see me do so."

"All right, captain."

Gliding cautiously down in the direction indicated, they

came at length to the seaward edge of the thicket, where the bushes, being less dense, permitted them to partially see the wreck. Here Dominick went on all-fours, appearing, as he crept slowly forward, like some sort of huge bear with no tail, and its hind feet turned the wrong way. Otto followed like a little bear with similar undignified peculiarities. Having advanced far enough to obtain a clear view of the wreck, the spies sank into the grass and crept forward a little way. Then they lay still a few moments and listened. They then raised their heads cautiously and looked. What they heard and saw puzzled them not a little.

First, they noted that the wreck did not seem to lie in the position, with which they had been so long familiar. Then, as their eyes became accustomed to the faint light, they observed that a small boat was moving busily about the vessel's bow, and that a group of dark scarce-distinguishable forms of men was standing on the shore. Presently there was heard a low, yet not unfamiliar growl. This was followed by a high yet not unfamiliar shriek, accompanied by a grating sound.

"Lions and cockatoos!" whispered Otto, who had crept up alongside of his brother by that time, "what *can* they be about?"

"Is that a line I see athwart the sky?" asked Dominick, "look—just between the wreck and the big ledge there."

Said Otto, "It's more than a line. *I* see it. Half a dozen lines at least, and something like a round lump in the middle of 'em. Don't you see it?—against the sky like a black moon—"

"Hush! boy—the growl again!"

"Ay, man, also the cockatoo."

R. M. Ballantyne

"Oh! I have it now," whispered Dominick, with a low laugh; "they've rove blocks and tackle from the ship to the rocks, and are working them softly. Evildoers fear to be overheard, even when there's no chance of being so! Your lion, Otto, is the subdued yo-heave-ho of the men."

"I see," said Otto, with a grin so broad that his white teeth glistened even in the dark, "and my cockatoo is the unsubdued screeching of the block-sheaves! They must be trying to get the ship off the reef."

A heavy plunge at that moment told that the conspirators were not only trying but had succeeded, for the plunge was followed by an irresistible though powerfully suppressed cheer.

"We have not a moment to lose, Otto," whispered Dominick. "The ship is free, and they will only take time to carry the tackle aboard before embarking. Do you run back and bring the squad down at the double. I will keep our friends here in play till they come."

Not a word did Otto reply. He had acquired that first of requisites in a soldier or servant—the habit of prompt obedience. Somewhat like a North American savage, he sank into the grass and wriggled from the scene. A few moments later Dominick rose, and walked down towards the conspirators with the easy off-hand manner of a man who saunters forth to enjoy the night air. So busy were they getting the tackle into the boat that he was not observed until quite close to them.

"You seem busy to-night, friends," he said, in his usual pleasant tones, as he took his stand close beside Hugh Morris, who was near the bow of the boat.

"Mr Rigonda!" exclaimed Malines in great surprise, coming forward at the moment.

"Why are you surprised? It is not unusual for me to take a row on a fine night."

This reply seeming to imply that Dominick had come to the reef alone—perhaps in the dinghy—emboldened the men; some of them laughed.

"Well, I confess to being a little surprised, sir," replied the mate, "for it so happened that we were preparing something in the nature of a surprise for you and the rest of the settlers."

"Yes, I see," returned Dominick, in the same pleasant tone. "You've managed to get the ship off the ledge in a very creditable manner, and you mean to take her into the lagoon and cast anchor off the settlement?"

Again the men laughed lightly.

"No, sir, we don't," broke in Hugh Morris at this point, "we intend to take her in quite the opposite direction, and clear off to sea with her."

"Oh no, you don't, Hugh," returned Dominick, with an agreeable smile, which was a little perplexing as well as exasperating. "You are going into the lagoon; you know you are, and I have come to help you."

"But I say we are *not*!" retorted Morris, in rising wrath, "and what's more, you'll have to go along with us, now that you've had the ill-luck to fall in with us."

"Quite right, Hugh; didn't I *say* that I came off on purpose to go along with you?"

As he spoke there was heard a rushing sound of feet and a number of dark forms were seen approaching from the bushes.

"Betrayed!" shouted Malines. "Jump in, lads, and shove off!"

He sprang forward, but was instantly arrested by the muzzle of a revolver within a foot of his head.

"It's of no use, boys," said Dominick, laying his hand on the bow of the boat. "You'll have to enter it as dead men if you do so without my permission."

Had the men been armed it might have gone hard with Dominick at that moment, but so sure had they been of accomplishing their purpose unmolested, that the idea of arming had never crossed their minds. Before they could recover from the surprise or decide what to do, the armed squad was upon them.

"Halt! boys," cried Joe Binney, when close to the boat. "Now, look 'ee here. It warn't o' my seekin' that I was made prime minister, but now that it's bin done I'll stick to it an' do my duty. If ye knock under like good boys I'll recommend ye to the queen's marcy. If not I'll have 'ee strung up, every man jack of 'ee. Moreover, the first man as disobeys my orders I'll blow his brains out. Now, jump aboard, boys (turning to his own men), an' keep your revolvers handy. You lads as wanted to run away will follow."

The mixture of humour and resolution in Joe's manner, coupled with his well-known decision of character and his commanding size, had its effect. The squad instantly jumped into the boat, and the conspirators meekly followed without a word. They saw—as Hugh afterwards expressed it—that the game was up, and made up their minds to submit to the inevitable.

The conspirators were ordered to take the oars. Afterwards they were made to work the ship round into the channel leading to the lagoon, while their armed friends mounted guard over them.

It was daybreak when the ship sailed calmly over the lagoon towards Silver Bay.

"Och! man," said Teddy Malone, in a low voice, to Jabez Jenkins, who stood near him, "why did ye want to run away wid the owld ship? It wor a sneakin' sort o' thing, warn't it, seein' that the poor little childers, an' the women, depind so much on what's inside of her?"

"To tell 'ee the truth, Teddy," replied the man, an improved expression coming suddenly over his face, "I ain't sorry that we've bin stopped in this business, and, wot's more, I believe that most of us ain't sorry. We was more than half led into it, d'ee see, by lies as to what the leaders was goin' to do, an' arterwards we didn't like to draw back."

"I'm sorry for yez," returned Malone, "for I'm afeared we'll have to skrag the wan half of ye to keep the other half in order. In a spik an' span noo settlement, where ivvery wan thinks he may do as he likes, the laws has to be pritty stiff. We've wan comfort, howivver—the quane is marciful."

The Irishman was right in both his views on this subject, as the sequel will show.

Great was the surprise and joy among the settlers that morning when the fine ship in which they had traversed the ocean sailed grandly over the lagoon, and let go her anchor in Silver Bay. Some viewed her as a means of continuing the voyage, and escaping from a secluded life, of which they were beginning to tire. Others thought of her as a means of reopening intercourse with home, while not a few thought only of the convenience of having her and her useful cargo so near to them.

But great was their surprise when Malines, Morris, Jabez, and the rest of them were landed with their hands bound behind their backs; and still greater was that surprise when, in open court, that is, in the midst of the entire colony in the open air, these men were charged with their crime.

A regular criminal court was instituted on the spot, as regular, at least, as was possible, considering the almost total ignorance of all concerned in regard to matters of law. Queen Pauline appointed Dr Marsh to be judge, he being supposed to be the best acquainted with, or least ignorant of, legal matters and forms. A jury of twelve men were selected by lot, and little Buxley was appointed public prosecutor. In justice to the prisoners it was thought that they ought to have an advocate to defend them, but as no one would undertake the duty, that also was settled by lot, and the lot fell upon Redding, who, being a gentle and meek man, was perhaps best suited for it.

We may not go into the details of this celebrated trial, which lasted the greater part of the day, and was watched with intense eagerness by the entire population, including some of the older children, who had become impressed with the delightfully-horrible idea that a hanging or shooting, if not flaying and roasting, of some of the criminals would be the certain result. Suffice it to say that there was grievous irregularity in the proceedings: the public prosecutor not only proved the guilt of the men, but in the fervour of his indignation suggested the nature of their punishment; the jury not only listened to the facts of the case, but commented on them freely throughout, and, usurping the judge's office, pronounced sentence on the criminals three or four times over; while the judge himself had the greatest possible difficulty in keeping anything like order all round.

The only man who performed his duty calmly was Redding, who, in a speech that quite surprised and transfixed the hearers, sought to point out that the men on trial had not actually committed the crime, with which they had been charged, that of seizing the ship, but had only contemplated it, as had been alleged, though even that had not been clearly proved; that, supposing the crime to have been committed, it was a first offence, and that justice should always be tempered with mercy, as was taught in that best of all law-books, the Bible.

The pleading of this man had considerable effect, but it could not turn the tide of feeling in favour of the principal prisoners for more than one reason. They had been domineering, turbulent fellows all along; they had meditated a crime which would have robbed the settlers of many of the necessaries and all the luxuries of life, and this displayed a meanness of spirit which, they thought, deserved severe punishment.

Accordingly, after they had been pronounced guilty by the unanimous voice of the jury, and after the judge had consulted earnestly with some members of the privy council, Malines and Morris were condemned to a fortnight's imprisonment on short allowance of the poorest food, and the other criminals to the same for a week.

When Malines had been seized and bound on board the ship, he had submitted, partly from prudence, and partly from a belief that the whole affair was a sort of half joke but when he found himself rebound, after the trial, and cast with his companions into a solid wooden building with a strong door and no window, which had been erected as a sort of fortress

R. M. Ballantyne

in which to put the women and children in case of attack by the savages, and there provided with maize and water for food and straw for bed, he began to realise the fact that he had indeed fallen into the hands of resolute men and under the power of law.

"I wouldn't mind it so much if they'd only not cut off our baccy," he groaned, on the afternoon of the following day, after a prolonged fit of sullen silence.

"After all it sarves us right," growled Hugh Morris.

"Speak for yourself," said Jabez Jenkins sulkily.

"That's just what I do," retorted Hugh.

"Hear, hear!" from some of the others.

What this conversation might have grown to no one can tell, for it was interrupted by the opening of the prison door and the entrance of a party of armed men.

"I am directed," said Otto, who was in command of the party, "to bring you fellows before the queen, so, come along."

Half amused by and half contemptuous of the leader, who gave his orders as if he were a powerful giant, the prisoners rose and marched out.

While this scene was taking place in the jail, the widow Lynch was holding a private interview with the queen in the palace.

CHAPTER ELEVEN

SHOWS HOW THE QUEEN CONDUCTED HERSELF IN TRYING CIRCUMSTANCES, AND WAS FINALLY DETHRONED

"Now, darlin'," said Mrs Lynch to Queen Pauline, as she sat on the side of her bed looking contemplatively at the floor, "thim rascals'll be in the Hall in two minits, so take me advice and give them more nor they've got."

"But my object in sending for them is not to add to their punishment," said the queen.

"More's the pity, for they need it, an' the Coort was too tinder wi' them intirely. Two weeks! why, two months would do them more good. Anyhow, see that ye give them a fearful blowin' up."

"I'll do what I can for them," returned Pina, with a pleasant laugh, as she rose and passed into the Audience Hall, where the prisoners and as many of the settlers as could find room were already gathered.

Here a slight change of feeling seemed to have taken place in the people. Perhaps the sight of Hugh and Malines—two men who had, up till that time, carried matters with rather a

R. M. Ballantyne

high hand—bound, humbled, helpless, and with bits of straw which had been given them as bedding sticking to their garments, induced a touch of pity. At all events, there was none of that riotous demand for vengeance which had characterised them when under the influence of excitement at the trial. Evidently a slight reaction in favour of the culprits had set in, and the entrance of the queen, therefore, took place in solemn silence, no one knowing why she had sent for the men or what were her intentions. Poor Pauline was much embarrassed by the silence, and by the situation, in which she found herself. Being a girl of mind, and not a mere human machine made and content to run always on beaten paths, she had resolved to try an experiment, and braced herself to the duty.

It was by no means a new experiment; on the contrary, it was older than this world's history, though new to Pauline in the particular circumstances—being an application of the law of mercy.

"My friends," said Pina, in a somewhat tremulous voice, which however became firmer as she proceeded, "this is the first trial that has taken place in our little colony, and as crime must be firmly repressed—"

("Punished, my dear—putt it stronger!" came in a whisper from the side door, where widow Lynch was listening; but, fortunately, none of the audience heard her.)

"I feel," continued Pauline, taking no notice of the advice, "that it becomes me, as your chosen queen, to do what I think will be best for the interests of the community."

"Hear, hear!" exclaimed some of the audience; but they gave no further expression to their feelings, being still uncertain as to the queen's leanings.

"No doubt," continued Pina, trying, not quite successfully, to swallow the lump in her throat, "the punishment which you have awarded these men is in strict accordance with your ideas of justice, and, being utterly ignorant of law, I will not presume to doubt the wisdom of your decision; nor would I interfere, either by increasing or decreasing the punishment, did I not feel that this case is peculiar, very peculiar. It is, as I have said, the beginning of crime in our kingdom, and little beginnings, you all know, often lead to great results. A small leak may sink a ship. Then, in the second place, this is the first offence committed by these men, and first offences require peculiar treatment—"

("That's so, my dear—*powerful* treatment. Give it 'em hot!" inaudibly whispered the widow.)

"Turning to that Book," continued Pauline, "which shall be my guide in every act of life, I find that God 'delighteth in mercy.' Can I go wrong in following humbly in His footsteps? I think not. Therefore, I venture to exercise the privilege of my position, and extend mercy to these men. The law has been vindicated by their trial and condemnation. I now, in accordance with constitutional right, bestow on them a free pardon."

This, being rapidly uttered, quite took the people by surprise, and caused them to burst into a ringing cheer, above which the no longer inaudible voice of the widow was heard to exclaim—

"Free parding, indeed!" in tones of indignant contempt, as she shut the door with a bang and retired in disgust from the scene.

"I do not know," said the queen, when silence was restored, "on what particular officer of my household," (a confused

R. M. Ballantyne

little smile and blush here), "falls the duty of setting crim—I mean *forgiven* men free, so I now order the prime minister to cut their bonds."

Amid some laughter, Joe readily drew forth an enormous clasp-knife and obeyed this command. Then the queen, stepping forward, held out her hand with a bright smile to Hugh Morris. None but an utterly abandoned wretch could have resisted that. Hugh gave in at once—seized the hand, and not only shook it, but kissed it heartily. So did Malines, and so did the others, and then they all dispersed—Teddy Malone signalling his exit with a cheer and a shout to the following effect—

"Hooroo! boys—she's ivvery inch a quane, an' two or three eighths over—cut an' dry, ready-made, hot off the irons! We're in luck—eh! boys, aren't we?"

The latter remark was made, with a hearty slap on the back, to little Buxley, who, turning at once and grasping Malone in his arms, went in for a vigorous wrestle by way of relieving his feelings.

Whatever may be thought of this matter by men deep in the learning of human law, we feel bound to put on record that this plan of Queen Pauline the First proved a great success, for, from that day forward, Malines and Morris and all the other conspirators became excellent members of the community—gave up all ideas of piracy on the high seas, set to work like men to fence in their properties, cultivate their farms, prosecute their fisheries, and otherwise to make themselves useful. Another result was that Silver Bay Settlement began to flourish.

Similar results usually happen when men give up quarrelling and take to working. The schoolroom was soon finished. The queen had her Bible classes—plenty of Bibles having been found in the ship—and Dominick even went the length of venturing to conduct special services on Sundays.

But, strange to say, the more things prospered on the island, the more pensive became the queen, as well as Otto and his brother. It was not so with Dr Marsh, however. Some unknown influence seemed to keep him always in a hearty frame of mind.

"I can't help it, Dom," said the queen, as she walked on the white shore of Silver Bay one evening while the sun was descending in a golden blaze, "I can't bear to think of them."

Poor Pauline's mind was running on a cheery bald little old gentleman in Java, and a mild little spectacled old lady, with knitting proclivities, in England, whose chief solace, in a humble way, was an elderly female cat.

"Am I *never* to see them again?" she added, as she sat down on a coral rock, buried her fair face in her hands, and wept.

Dominick tried to comfort her, but in vain.

"It's all very well what you say, Dom, but here we are settling down as if we meant to stay for ever. Even Otto talks less than he used to about Robinson Crusoe, and no ships ever come near us, and the sailors don't want to quit the islands, so we can't even use the ship we have got, and—and—O darling mother! and dear, *dear* papa!"

If Queen Pina, who broke down at this point, had only known that, about the time she was speaking, the *dear* papa was running for his life, covered with mud from head to foot, in the midst of thunder and fire and smoke, she might have mingled horror with loving emphasis as she mentioned his name.

At the time of which we write, the island of Java, in the Malay Archipelago, was convulsed by one of those tremendous earthquakes which have at irregular intervals, from time immemorial, shattered its mountains, over-whelmed some of its fairest lands, and killed thousands of its inhabitants. It is not our intention, however, to touch on this subject more than will suffice to elucidate our tale.

Deeply interesting is it, at times, to note the intimate connection that sometimes exists between places and events which seem exceedingly remote. One would imagine that the eruption of a volcanic mountain in Java could not have much influence on the life or fortunes of people living on an island nearly a thousand miles distant from the same. Yet so it was, in a double sense, too, as we shall see.

The great shock in Java, which overturned the bald little old gentleman's chair, causing him to spring up and exclaim to his partner, "Hallo, Brooks!" passed through the intervening earth, losing much of its power on the way, caused Refuge Islands to tremble, and Pauline to look up suddenly with the exclamation—

"What's that Dom?"

"It is marvellously like an earthquake, Pina."

Strange to say, Brooks in Java made precisely the same remark, at about the same moment, to his senior partner.

Thereafter old Mr Rigonda, who didn't like earthquakes, said to Brooks—who didn't mind earthquakes, being used to them—

"I'll start off for England immediately."

He did start off, even more immediately than he had intended, for the neighbouring volcano, as if angered by his remark, sent up a shock that shook the surrounding houses to their foundations. The senior partner rushed out in terror, and was just in time to receive a shower of mud and ashes while he fled away through fire and smoke, as already mentioned.

The volcano went to sleep again for a short time after that little indication of its power, and you may be sure that old Rigonda did not wait for its reawakening. One of his own ships was on the point of sailing that very day. He went on board—after cleaning himself—got Brooks to wind up their business relations in the cabin, and left for England with a fair wind.

And well was it for the bald little old gentleman that he did so, for, a few days later, strange sounds and appearances were in the air and on the sea. Fine ashes filled the sky, so that noon became like midnight, and everything betokened that something unusually violent must have occurred in the land which they had left. Nothing more serious, however, befell our voyager. In due course he reached England, hastened home, and, without warning, burst in upon his wife while that dear little old lady was in the act of remarking to the middle-aged cat, in a very dolorous tone, that she feared something must have happened to the ship, for her darlings could never have been so long of writing if all had gone well.

It was while the cat gazed contemplatively at the everlasting socks, as if meditating a reply, that old Rigonda burst in.

Starting up with amazing activity and a cry of joy, the old lady swept her feline friend from the table—inadvertently, of course—and rushed into her husband's arms, while the outraged animal sought refuge on top of the bookcase, whence it glared at the happy meeting with feelings that may

R. M. Ballantyne

be more easily understood than described. Of course the old man's joy was turned into grief and anxiety when he heard of the departure of his children and was told of their prolonged silence; but with that we have nothing to do at present.

We return to Silver Bay, where a sense of insecurity had been aroused in the community, ever since the tremors of the earth, to which we have just referred.

With the slumbering of the Javanese mountains, however, these tremors and the consequent fears subsided, and were almost forgotten in another source of anxiety.

One morning, while Teddy Malone was walking on the beach of Silver Bay, he observed a small object running and stumbling towards him, as if in great haste or fear. Hurrying forward to meet this object he soon perceived that it was little Brown-eyes, of whom he was very fond.

"What's wrong, me darlint?" he asked, catching the child up and kissing her.

"Oh, such funny tings me sawd—oder side de rocks," replied Brown-eyes, panting; "come wid me an' see dem. Come kik!"

"Funny things, eh, mavourneen, what sort of things?"

"Oh, like beasts. Come kik!"

"They wasn't sarpints, was they?" said Malone, seating the child on his shoulder and hastening towards the rocky point which separated Silver Bay from the land beyond.

"No, no—not saa'pints. Long beasts, like mans, only hims not stand and walk, but lie down and crawl."

Much impressed with the child's eager manner, the Irishman hurried towards the point of rocks, filled with curiosity as to what the creatures could be.

"What sort o' hids have they, darlint?" he asked, as he neared the point.

"Hids same as mans, and faces like you, but more uglier, all scratched over, an' dey try to catch me, but me runned away."

Teddy Malone's hitherto obtuse faculties were awakened. He stopped suddenly, being by that time convinced that he stood unarmed within spear-throw of savages in ambush. To advance, supposing his conjecture to be right, he knew would be certain death. To turn and fly would probably be the same, for naked savages could easily overtake him even if unburdened with Brown-eyes, whom, of course, he could not forsake, and he was too far from the settlement to shout an alarm.

Perspiration burst from poor Teddy's brow, for even delay, he knew, would be fatal, as the savages would suspect him of having discovered them.

Suddenly he put Brown-eyes down on the sand, and, twisting his figure into a comical position, began to hop like a frog. His device had the desired effect; Brown-eyes burst into a hearty fit of laughter, forgot for the moment the "funny beasts," and cried, "Do it agin!"

The poor man did it again, thinking intensely all the time what he should do next.

"Would you like to see me dance, darlint?" he asked suddenly.

R. M. Ballantyne

"Oh yis!"

Thereupon Teddy Malone began to dance an Irish jig to his own whistling, although, being much agitated, he found it no easy matter to whistle in tune or time, but that was unimportant. As he danced he took care to back in a homeward direction. The child naturally followed. Thus, by slow degrees, he got beyond what he considered spear-throw, and feeling boldness return with security, he caught the child up and danced with her on his shoulder. Then he set her down, and pretended to chase her. He even went the length of chasing her a little way in the wrong direction, in order to throw the savages more completely off their guard. By degrees he got near to the settlement, and there was met by Otto.

"You seem jolly to-day, Ted," said the boy.

"Whist, lad," returned the other, without intermitting his exercise. "Look as if ye was admirin' me. There's lot of them tattooed monkeys—savages—beyant the pint. They don't know I've found it out. Slink up an' gather the boys, an' look alive. I'll amuse 'em here till you come back. An' I say, don't forgit to bring me revolver an' cutlash."

"All right," was Otto's brief reply, as he sauntered slowly up towards the bushes. No sooner was he screened by these, however, than he ran like a hare to the palace.

"Halloo! Dom, Joe, Hugh—all of you—the savages again! Arm—quick!"

It needed no urging to hasten the movements of all who heard the boy's voice. Ever since the first appearance of the savages Dominick and the doctor had put all the men of the settlement under daily training in drill for an hour or so, that they might be better able to act promptly and in concert if occasion should again occur. The arms had been collected, and such of them as were not in use stored in a handy position, so that in two minutes an armed company was proceeding at a run towards the spot on the shore where Malone was still performing his antics, to the inexpressible delight of Brown-eyes.

"Where are the spalpeens?" asked the widow Lynch, who had followed the men.

"Beyant the rocks, mother," answered Malone, as he received his weapons from Otto and fell into his place in the ranks; "ye'd as well take the child home, or she'll be sure to follow—she's nigh as wild as yerself."

The widow was indeed fond of seeing, as she used to say, "all the fun that was goin'," but on this occasion she consented to carry Brown-eyes out of danger while the settlers moved at a quick step towards the point.

Behind that point of rocks a band of savages lay concealed, as Malone had rightly conjectured. There were about forty of them, all armed with clubs and spears, evidently bent on attacking the settlement. Of course they meant to do it by surprise, and had concealed themselves among the bushes behind the point, where they probably would have lain till nightfall if Brown-eyes in her wanderings had not discovered them. Their chief would have instantly caught and silenced the poor child, had she not run so far clear of the point that he would infallibly have revealed himself to Teddy Malone in doing so.

When that worthy drew near to the rocks, as described, the chief got ready a spear for his reception. When Malone took to dancing, the chief condescended to smile, or grin, hideously. When he retreated out of range the chief consoled himself with the reflection that it was just as well, night being the best time for attack. When, however, he beheld a band of men moving towards him armed with the terrible things that "spouted smoke, fire, and stones," a change came over the spirit of his dream. After a hasty consultation with his comrades, he glided off in the direction of their canoe. The rest followed, and when our settlers at last turned the point, they saw the foe paddling at full speed across the lagoon.

Firing a volley of disappointment after them, both in words and bullets, they ran to their boats and gave chase, but, as on the former occasion, the canoe proved too swift for the boats under oars, and the savages got away.

The anxiety that naturally filled the breasts of Queen Pauline and her councillors at this event was speedily forgotten in a recurrence of the earthquake which had previously alarmed them so much.

It happened on a calm, bright morning, when the widow Lynch chanced to be washing garments in the palace beside the queen. You see they had not much regard for state-ceremonial or etiquette at the court of Pauline the First even in public, much less in private, so that, while the widow was deep in the washtub at one end of the hall, the queen was busy at the other end patching Otto's garments.

At first there occurred a slight trembling of the earth, which the widow, attributing to giddiness in her own cranium, recognised with a remonstrative "Ohone!"

"Did you feel *that*?" exclaimed Pauline, pausing in her work and looking up with a slight feeling of alarm.

"*What*, dearie?" demanded the widow, clearing the soap-suds from her red roly-poly arms.

Before Pauline could answer, the earthquake took the liberty of reply by giving an abrupt shake to the whole island, which not only set chairs and tables rocking in an alarming manner, but drove the entire population from their houses in consternation. Among other effects it caused Mrs Lynch to stagger and catch hold of the washtub, which, far from supporting her, let her fall to the ground, and fell on the top of her.

To most of the settlers the sensation of a trembling earth was quite new and exceedingly alarming. They stopped abruptly after the first rush, and then looked about with pale faces, not knowing what to do. Malines, however, was cool and collected. He had been in various volcanic regions of the world, and undertook to comfort them.

"Don't be afraid," he said, when the most of the people had gathered round him. "I've often seen this sort o' thing, on the coast o' South America and among the Malay Islands. It passes away after a while, and often without doin' much damage—though I *have* seen a town shook almost to pieces in about five minutes."

"And what did they do?" asked Jabez Jenkins.

"Och, whirri-hoo!" shouted Teddy Malone, for at that moment another shock was felt, more violent than the preceding. The earth seemed absolutely to roll, and one or two of the huts that had been carelessly built, fell asunder in partial ruin.

"Where is my brother—and the doctor?" demanded Pauline, running up to the group at the moment.

"They're away up the mountain, with Joe and Otto," answered little Buxley; "I saw 'em start soon after daybreak—to explore, they said."

"What do you think should be done?" asked Pina, turning naturally to the mate, as being the most intelligent of those around her.

"If it's goin' to be bad," said Malines, "I would advise you all to git on board the ship as fast as ye can, for the land isn't so safe as the water when it takes to quakin'."

"You seem to have had some experience of it. Is it going to be bad, think you?"

"Earthquakes are deceptive—no man can tell."

"Well, then, we must do our best at once," said the queen, with an air of calm decision worthy of her rank. "Go, Mr Malines, with your sailors, and get all the boats ready. And you, my people, carry down what you esteem most valuable and get on board the ship without loss of time—for the rest, we are in the hands of a loving and merciful God."

While these events were enacting on the shore, Dominick, Otto, the doctor, and Joe Binney were seated near the summit of the highest peak, enjoying a cold breakfast. It was their first visit to that particular peak, which had a slight hollow or basin of perhaps fifty feet diameter in the centre.

Just before the first tremulous shock the doctor had been explaining to the prime minister the nature of volcanoes, and stating his opinion that the cup-like hollow before them was an extinct crater. The slight shock stopped him in his discourse, and caused the party to look at each other with serious faces.

"It's not extinct yet," exclaimed Otto excitedly, pointing to the hollow, the earth of which had suddenly cracked in several places and was emitting puffs of sulphurous smoke and steam.

They all started up.

"We'd better hasten home," said Dominick.

"Yes—they'll be terribly scared," said the doctor, hastily beginning to pack up the remains of their breakfast.

But, before this could be done, the second convulsion took place. Violent trembling occurred for a few seconds; then the ground in the old crater burst open, and, with a terrible explosion, fire and smoke belched forth, sending huge fragments of rock and showers of ashes into the air, which latter fell around the explorers in all directions—fortunately without doing them injury.

They waited no longer. Without even uttering a word they all turned and ran down the hill at full speed. Being a considerable distance from the settlement, it was upwards of an hour before they arrived. By that time most of the women and children had been sent off to the ship. Pauline, however, had remained on shore to direct and encourage the rest, as well as to await the return of her brothers.

"Right—right—you couldn't have done better," said Dominick, when Pauline hastily explained how she had acted.

"It was Mr Malines, not I, who suggested the plan," returned the queen.

"Hadn't you better go on board yourself?" said the doctor, "and leave us to manage."

"No, I am not a mere puppet, sir," answered Pauline, with a little smile, yet firmly. "My place is here till all my subjects are safe! And your duty is to assist in the embarkation, not to offer advice to your queen!"

With a laugh the doctor went off to do his duty, muttering, "My *queen*, indeed!" fervently.

For some time the volcano, which had thus sprung into sudden activity, partially subsided, yet there were occasional tremulous motions of the earth and low growlings in the heart of the mountain on Big Island, while several minor explosions occurred in the crater, so that the thoroughly alarmed settlers hastened the embarkation with all despatch. Before night had closed in they were all safely on board with most of their lighter valuables and tools, though, necessarily, much of their heavier property was left behind. Where life is threatened, however, men are not apt to mind such losses.

It now became a question whether they should remain at anchor where they were and abide the issue, or proceed at once to sea. Some were for remaining, others were for putting off to sea. There was much wrangling over it at first, and the people seemed in their anxiety to have quite forgotten their queen, when she stepped forward, and, raising her clear silvery voice, produced a dead calm at once.

"Joe," she said, "go down to the cabin and await me there."

The prime minister obeyed instantly.

"Now," said Pauline, turning to the people, "choose among you six of your number to consult with me, and do it at once."

Of course, the men well-known as the best among the settlers were instantly named we need scarcely add that among them were Dominick, the doctor, and Malines.

While these were engaged in consultation below, a terrible outburst of the volcano settled the matter for them, and brought them all hastily on deck.

The summit of the crater seemed to have been blown up into the air with a most terrific noise, while a dense mass of smoke, steam, and ashes was hurled upwards, and seemed to blot out the sky. Twilight, which had been deepening, was converted into blackest night in a moment, and darkness profound would undoubtedly have continued, had it not been for the lurid glare of the fires which flashed at intervals from the crater. Suddenly the waters of the sea became agitated. The ship rocked uneasily, and jerked at her cable, while the terrified people clung to shrouds and ropes, and belaying-pins. Then the fire on the mountain-top increased tenfold in volume and intensity. Another moment, and several large holes opened in the mountain-side nearest to them, from which streams of molten lava burst forth and began to descend towards the deserted settlement.

At that moment there was a great shout. It had been discovered that in the confusion little Brown-eyes had been forgotten!

A small boat hung at the davits on the port side. It was manned instantly. The doctor jumped to the helm, Otto followed, and, before any could interpose, the queen suddenly stepped in.

"You are mad!" cried the doctor.

"Lower away!" said Pina, as if she had been a trained sea-captain all her life.

Instantly the ropes were eased off, and in a few seconds the boat was in the sea and on the shore. They found little Brown-eyes sound asleep in her crib, with a river of red-hot lava stretching its fiery tongues towards her as if eager for a meal!

Supple-limbed Otto was first; he seized the child and bore her off to the boat. Another terrible explosion occurred just then. Ashes and masses of rock began to rain around them. A falling stone struck Pauline's head, and she fell. The doctor, who held her hand, seized her in his arms and bore her away. A few minutes more and they were all safe on board again.

But there was no time for congratulations. The sea which had before been agitated, now heaved in wild waves, though there was no wind. It was then seen that Big Island was actually crumbling—sinking into the water! The continuous rumbling of the volcano was terrible. Intermittent explosions were frequent. To add to the horrors of the scene the darkness deepened. As the island went down the sea rushed tumultuously in to overwhelm it. Then it was that the stout cable, under God, saved them from immediate destruction. The ship was hurled from side to side like a cork on the boiling flood. But no cable could long withstand such a strain. The chain snapped at last, and they seemed to be rushing with railway speed to their fate amid surrounding fire and overwhelming water, and roaring thunders, and raining ashes, when, suddenly, there was a perceptible diminution in the turmoil, and, gradually, the waves calmed down. With feelings of intense thankfulness the terrified people let go their second anchor, though the darkness was by that time so thick that they could barely see each other.

It may be imagined what a night of anxiety they spent. With Pauline and some others it was a night of earnest prayer.

When the light of day at last broke faintly in the east it revealed the fact that Refuge Islands had actually and totally disappeared, and that our settlers were floating on the bosom of the open sea!

R. M. Ballantyne

CHAPTER TWELVE

LAST CHAPTER

An Island Queen no longer, Pauline Rigonda sits on the quarter-deck of the emigrant ship gazing pensively over the side at the sunlit sea. Dethroned by the irresistible influences of fire and water, our heroine has retired into the seclusion of private life.

After escaping from the volcano, as described in the last chapter, the settlers resolved to proceed, under the guidance of Malines as captain, and Morris as mate, to the port for which they had originally been bound when the disaster on Refuge Islands had arrested them.

Of course this was a great disappointment to poor Pauline and her brothers, who, as may be imagined, were burning with anxiety to get back to England. Feeling, however, that it would be unreasonable as well as selfish to expect the emigrants to give up their long-delayed plans merely to meet their wishes, they made up their minds to accept the situation with a good grace.

"You see," said Otto to the ex-queen—for he was becoming very wise in his own eyes, and somewhat oracular in the midst of all these excitements—"when a fellow can't help himself he's bound to make the best of a bad business."

"Don't you think it would be better to say he is bound to accept trustingly what God arranges, believing that it will be all for the best?" returned Pauline.

"How can a bad business be for the best?" demanded Otto, with the air of one who has put an unanswerable question.

His sister looked at him with an expression of perplexity. "Well, it is not easy to explain," she said, "yet I can believe that all *is* for the best."

"Ha, Pina!" returned the boy, with a little touch of pride, "it's all very well for you to say that, but you won't get men to believe things in that way."

"Otto," said Dr Marsh, who was standing near and listening to the conversation, "it is not so difficult as you think to prove that what we call a bad business may after all be for the best. I remember at this moment a case in point. Come— I'll tell you a story. Once upon a time I knew a gentleman with a stern face and a greedy soul, who believed in nothing, almost, except in the wickedness of mankind, and in his own capacity to take advantage of that wickedness in order to make money. Money was his god. He spent all his time and all his strength in making it, and he was successful. He had many ships on the sea, and much gold in the bank. He had also a charming little wife, who prayed in secret that God would deliver her husband from his false god, and he had a dear little daughter who loved him to distraction in spite of his 'business habits!' Well, one year there came a commercial crisis. Mr Getall eagerly risked his money and over-speculated. That same year was disastrous in the way of storms and wrecks. Among the wrecks were several of Mr Getall's finest ships. A fire reduced one of his warehouses to

R. M. Ballantyne

ashes, and, worse still, one of his most confidential and trusted clerks absconded with some thousands of pounds. All that was a very bad business, wasn't it?"

"It was," assented Otto; "go on."

"The upshot was a crash—"

"What!—of the burning warehouse?"

"No; of the whole business, and the Getalls were reduced to comparative beggary. The shock threw the poor little wife, who had always been rather delicate, into bad health, rendering a warm climate necessary for her at a time when they could not afford to travel. Moreover, little Eva's education was entirely stopped at perhaps the most important period of her life. That was a bad business, wasn't it?"

"That was a much worse business," asserted Otto.

"Well, when Mr Getall was at the lowest stage of despair, and had taken more than one look over the parapet of London Bridge with a view to suicide, he received a letter from a long-neglected brother, who had for many years dwelt on the Continent, partly for economy and partly for a son's health. The brother offered him a home in the south of France for the winter, as it would do his wife good, he said, and he had room in his house for them all, and wanted their company very much to keep him from being dull in that land of warmth and sunshine! Getall was not the man to refuse such an offer. He went. The brother was an earnest Christian. His influence at that critical time of sore distress was the means in the Holy Spirit's hands of rescuing the miser's soul, and transferring his heart from gold to the Saviour. A joy which he had never before dreamed of took possession of him, and he began, timidly at first to commend Jesus to others. Joy, they say, is curative. The effect of her husband's conversion did so much good to little Mrs Getall's spirit that her body began steadily to mend, and in time she was restored to better health than she had enjoyed in England. The brother-in-law, who was a retired schoolmaster, undertook the education of Eva, and, being a clever man as well as good, trained her probably much better than she would have been trained had she remained at home. At last they returned to England, and Mr Getall, with the assistance of friends, started afresh in business. He never again became a rich man in the worldly sense, but he became rich enough to pay off all his creditors to the last farthing; rich enough to have something to spare for a friend in distress; rich enough to lay past something for Eva's dower, and rich enough to contribute liberally to the funds of those whose business it is to 'consider the poor.' All that, you see, being the result of what you have admitted, my boy, was a bad business."

"True, but then," objected Otto, who was of an argumentative turn, "if all that *hadn't* resulted, it would have been a bad business still."

"Not necessarily—it might have turned out to be a good business in some other way, or for somebody else. The mere fact that we can't see how, is no argument against the theory that *everything* is constrained to work for good by Him who rules the universe."

"What! even sin?" asked Otto, in surprise.

"Even sin," returned the doctor. "Don't you see that it was Getall's sin of greed and over-speculation, and the clerk's sin of embezzlement, which led to all these good results; but, of course, as neither of them had any desire or intention to achieve the good results which God brought about, they were none the less guilty, and were entitled to no credit, but, on

R. M. Ballantyne

the contrary, to condign punishment. What I wish to prove is that God causes *all things* to work out His will, yet leaves the free-will of man untouched. This is a great mystery; at the same time it is a great fact, and therefore I contend that we have every reason to trust our loving Father, knowing that whatever happens to us will be for the best—not, perhaps, for our present pleasure or gratification, but for our ultimate best."

"But—but—but," said Otto, while premature wrinkles rippled for a minute over his smooth brow, "at that rate, is it fair to blame sinners when their very sins are made to bring about God's will?"

"Now, Otto, don't run away with a false idea. For you to sin with a view to bring about good, is one thing—and a very wicked thing, which is severely condemned in Scripture—but for God to cause good to result from your sin, and in spite of *you*, is a totally different thing. Think of a pirate, my boy, a bloody-handed villain, who has spent his life of crime in gathering together enormous wealth, with which to retire into selfish enjoyment at last. But he is captured. His wealth is taken from him, and with it good men establish almshouses for the aged poor, hospitals for the sick, free libraries and free baths everywhere, and many other good and beneficent works. The pirate's labours have, in God's providence, been turned into this channel. Is the pirate less guilty, or less deserving of punishment on that account?"

Further discussion on this point was interrupted by a sharp order from Malines to reduce sail, and the consequent bustling about of the sailors.

"Going to blow, think you?" asked Dominick, who came on deck at the moment.

"Can't tell yet," replied the mate, "but the glass has fallen suddenly, and one must be prepared, all the more that the ship has been more severely strained on the reef than I had thought. Would Miss Pauline be prepared," he added in a lower tone, "to receive the deputation this afternoon?"

"Yes, she is quite prepared," returned Dominick, in the same low tone, "though she is much perplexed, not being able to understand what can be wanted of her. Is it so profound a secret that I may not know it?"

"You shall both know it in good time," the mate replied, as he turned to give fresh directions to the man at the wheel.

That afternoon the assembly in the cabin could hardly be styled a deputation, for it consisted of as many of the emigrants as could squeeze in. It was led by Joe Binney, who stood to the front with a document in his hand. Pauline, with some trepidation and much surprise expressed on her pretty face, was seated on the captain's chair, with an extra cushion placed thereon to give it a more throne-like dignity. She was supported by Dominick on one side and Otto on the other.

Joe advanced a few paces, stooping his tall form, partly in reverence and partly to avoid the deck-beams. Clearing his throat, and with a slightly awkward air, he read from the document as follows:—

"Dear Miss Pauline, may it please yer majesty, for we all regards you yet as our lawful queen, I've bin appinted, as prime minister of our community—which ain't yet broke up—to express our wishes, likewise our sentiments."

"That's so—go it, Joe," broke in a soft whisper from Teddy Malone.

"We wishes, first of all," continued the premier, "to say as how we're very sorry that your majesty's kingdom has bin blowed up an' sunk to the bottom o' the sea," ("Worse luck!" from Mrs Lynch),—"but we congratulate you an' ourselves that we, the people, are all alive,"—("an' kickin'," softly, from Malone—"Hush!" "silence!" from several others),— "an' as loyal an' devoted as ever we was." ("More so," and "Hear, hear!"). "Since the time you, Queen Pauline, took up the reins of guvermint, it has bin plain to us all that you has done your best to rule in the fear o' God, in justice, truthfulness, an' lovin' kindness. An' we want to tell you, in partikler, that your readin's out of the Bible to us an' the child'n—which was no part o' your royal dooty, so to speak—has done us all a power o' good, an' there was some of us big uns as needed a lot o' good to be done us, as well as the child'n—" ("Sure an' that's true, annyhow!" from Teddy).

"Now, what we've got to say," continued Joe, clearing his throat again, and taking a long breath, "is this—the land we're agoin' to ain't thickly popilated, as we knows on, an' we would take it kindly if you'd consent to stop there with us, an' continue to be our queen, so as we may all stick together an' be rightly ruled on the lines o' lovin' kindness,"—("With a taste o' the broomstick now an' then," from Teddy). "If your majesty agrees to this, we promise you loyal submission an' sarvice. Moreover, we will be glad that your brother, Mister Dominick, should be prime minister, an' Mister Otto his scritairy, or wotever else you please. Also that Dr Marsh should be the chansler o' the checkers, or anything else you like, as well as sawbones-in-gineral to the community. An' this our petition," concluded Joe, humbly laying the document at Pauline's feet, "has bin signed by every man in the ship—except Teddy Malone—"

"That's a lie!" shouted the amazed Teddy.

"Who," continued Joe, regardless of the interruption, "not bein' able to write, has put his cross to it."

"Hear, hear!" cried the relieved Irishman, while the rest laughed loudly—but not long, for it was observed that Pauline had put her handkerchief to her eyes.

What the ex-queen said in reply, we need not put down in detail. Of course, she expressed her gratitude for kind expressions, and her thankfulness for what had been said about her Sabbath-school work. She also explained that her dear mother in England, as well as their old father in Java, must be filled with deepest anxiety on account of herself and her brothers by that time, and that, therefore, she was obliged, most unwillingly, to decline the honour proposed to her.

"Och!" exclaimed the disappointed widow Lynch, "cudn't ye sind for yer mother to come out to yez, an' the ould man in Javy too? They'd be heartily welcome, an' sure we'd find 'em some sitivation under guvermint to kape their pot bilin'."

But these strong inducements failed to change the ex-queen's mind.

Now, while this was going on in the cabin, a change was taking place in the sky. The bad weather which Malines had predicted came down both suddenly and severely, and did the ship so much damage as to render refitting absolutely necessary. There was no regular port within hundreds of miles of them, but Malines said he knew of one of the eastern isles where there was a safe harbour, good anchorage, and plenty of timber. It would not take long to get there, though, considering the damaged state of the ship, it might take some months before they could get her into a fit state to continue the voyage. Accordingly, they altered their

R. M. Ballantyne

course, with heavy hearts, for the emigrants were disappointed at having their voyage again interrupted, while the Rigondas were depressed at the thought of the prolonged anxiety of their parents.

"Now this *is* a bad business, isn't it?" said Otto to the doctor, with a groan, when the course was decided.

"Looks like it, my boy; but it isn't," replied the doctor, who nevertheless, being himself but a frail mortal, was so depressed that he did not feel inclined to say more.

In this gloomy state of matters Pina's sweet tones broke upon them like a voice from the better land—as in truth it was— saying, "I will trust and not be afraid."

About this time the cloud which hung over the emigrant ship was darkened still more by a visit from the Angel of Death. The mother of Brown-eyes died. At that time Pauline was indeed an angel of mercy to mother and child. After the remains of the mother were committed to the deep, the poor orphan clung so piteously to Pauline that it was scarcely possible to tear her away. It was agreed at last that, as the child had now no natural protector, except an uncle and aunt, who seemed to think they had already too many children of their own, Pauline should adopt her.

When the emigrants reached the island-harbour, without further mishap, they were surprised to find a large steamer at anchor. The captain of it soon explained that extensive damage to the machinery had compelled him to run in there for shelter while the necessary repairs were being effected.

"Where are you bound for?" asked Dominick, who with Dr Marsh and Otto had accompanied Malines on board the steamer.

"For England."

"For England?" almost shouted Dominick and Otto in the same breath.

"Yes. Our repairs are completed, we set off to-morrow."

"Have you room for two or three passengers?"

"Yes, plenty of room. We shall have to put several ashore at the Cape, where I hope to get a doctor, too, for our doctor died soon after we left port, and we are much in want of one, having a good many sick men on board."

"Otto," whispered Dr Marsh, "our having been diverted from our course has not turned out such a bad business after all, has it?"

"On the contrary, the very best that could have happened. I'll never give way to unbelief again!"

Poor Otto! He did not at that time know how deeply doubt and unbelief are ingrained in the human heart. He did not know that man has to be convinced again and again, and over again, before he learns to hope against hope, and to believe heartily at all times that, "He doeth all things well."

It was with very mingled feelings that the Rigondas, Dr Marsh, and Brown-eyes parted next day from the friends with whom they had associated so long. It is no exaggeration to say that there was scarcely a dry eye in the two vessels; for, while the settlers wept for sorrow, the crews and passengers wept more or less from sympathy. Even the dead-eyes of the ship, according to Malone, shed tears! As for poor Brown-eyes, who was a prime favourite with many of her old friends, male and female, before she got away she had been almost crushed out of existence by strong arms, and her eyes might have been pea-green or pink for anything you could tell, so lost were they in the swollen lids. Long after the vessels had separated the settlers continued to shout words of good-will and blessing, "We'll never forgit ye, Miss Pauline," came rolling after them in the strong tones of Joe Binney. "God bless you, Miss," came not less heartily from Hugh Morris. "We loves ye, darlint," followed clear and shrill from the vigorous throat of the widow Lynch, and a wild "Hooray!" from Teddy endorsed the sentiment. Nobbs, the blacksmith, and little Buxley, ran up the rigging to make the waving of their caps more conspicuous, and when faces could no longer be distinguished and voices no longer be heard, the waving of kerchiefs continued until the rounding of a cape suddenly shut them all out from view for ever.

"Thank God," said Dr Marsh, with a voice deepened and tremulous from emotion, "that though they have lost their queen, they shall never lose the sweet influences she has left behind her."

The great ocean steamer had now cleared the land; her mighty engines seemed to throb with joy at being permitted once more to, "Go ahead, full speed," and soon she was cleaving her way grandly through the broad-backed billows of the Southern sea—homeward bound!

Let us leap on in advance of her.

The little old lady with the gold spectacles and neat black cap, and smooth, braided hair, is seated in her old arm-chair, with the old sock, apparently—though it must have been the latest born of many hundreds of socks—on the needles, and the unfailing cat at her elbow. The aspect of the pair gives the impression that if a French Revolution or a Chili earthquake were to visit England they would click-and-gaze on with imperturbable serenity through it all.

But the little old lady is not alone now. Old Mr Rigonda sits at the table opposite to her, with his forehead in his hands, as though he sought to squeeze ideas into his head from a book which lies open before him on the table. Vain hope, for the book is upside down. Profound silence reigns, with the exception of the clicking needles and the purring cat.

"My dear," at length exclaimed the bald old gentleman, looking up with a weary sigh.

"Yes, John?" (Such is his romantic Christian name!)

"I can't stand it, Maggie." (Such is *her* ditto!)

"It is, indeed, hard to bear, John. If we only knew for certain that they are—are gone, it seems as if we could bow to His will; but this terrible and wearing uncertainty is awful. Did you make inquiry at Lloyd's to-day?"

"Lloyd's? You seem to think Lloyd's can tell everything about all that happens on the sea. No, it's of no use inquiring anywhere, or doing anything. We can only sit still and groan."

In pursuance of this remaining consolation, the poor old gentleman groaned heavily and squeezed his forehead tighter, and gazed at the reversed book more sternly, while the old lady heaved several deep sighs. Even the cat introduced a feeble mew, as of sympathy, into the midst of its purr—the hypocrite!

"It was the earthquake that did it," cried Mr Rigonda, starting up, and pacing the room wildly, "I'm convinced of that."

R. M. Ballantyne

"How can that be, John, dear, when you were in Java at the time, and our darlings were far away upon the sea?"

"How can *I* tell how it could be, Maggie? Do you take me for a geological philosopher, who can give reasons for every earthly thing he asserts? All I know is that these abominable earthquakes go half through the world sometimes. Pity they don't go through the other half, split the world in two, and get rid of the subterranean fires altogether."

"John, my dear!"

"Well, Maggie, don't be hard on me for gettin' irascible now and then. If you only knew what I suffer when—but forgive me. You *do* know what I suffer—there!"

He stooped and kissed the old lady's forehead. The cat, uncertain, apparently, whether an assault was meant, arched its back and tall, and glared slightly. Seeing however that nothing more was done, it subsided.

Just then the wheels of a cab were heard rattling towards the front door, as if in haste. The vehicle stopped suddenly. Then there was impatient thundering at the knocker, and wild ringing of the bell.

"Fire!" gasped the half-petrified Mrs Rigonda.

"No smell!" said her half-paralysed spouse.

Loud voices in the passage; stumbling feet on the stairs; suppressed female shrieks; bass masculine exclamations; room door burst open; old couple, in alarm, on their feet; cat, in horror, on the top of the bookcase!

"Mother! mother! O father!"—yelled, rather than spoken.

Another moment, and the bald, little old man was wrestling in the ex-queen's arms; the little old lady was engulfed by Dominick and Otto; Dr John Marsh and Brown-eyes stood transfixed and smiling with idiotic joy at the door; while the cat—twice its size, with every hair erect—glared, and evolved miniature volcanoes in its stomach.

It was an impressive sight. Much too much so to dwell on!

Passing it over, let us look in on that happy home when toned down to a condition of reasonable felicity.

"It's a dream—all a wild, unbelievable dream!" sighed the old gentleman, as, with flushed face and dishevelled hair, he spread himself out in an easy chair, with Queen Pina on his knee and Brown-eyes at his feet. "Hush! all of you—wait a bit."

There was dead silence, and some surprise for a few seconds, while Mr Rigonda shut his eyes tight and remained perfectly still, during which brief lull the volcanic action in the cat ceased, and its fur slowly collapsed.

"Dreams shift and change so!" murmured the sceptical man, gradually opening his eyes again—"What! you're there yet, Pina?"

"Of course I am, darling daddy."

"Here, pinch me on the arm, Dominick—the tender part, else I'll not waken up sufficiently to dispel it."

A fresh outburst of hilarity, which started the stomachic volcanoes and hair afresh, while Pauline flung her arms round her father's neck for the fiftieth time, and smothered him. When he was released, and partially recovered, Otto

R. M. Ballantyne

demanded to know if he really wanted the dream dispelled.

"Certainly not, my boy, certainly not, if it's real; but it would be so dreadfully dismal to awake and find you all gone, that I'd prefer to dream it out, and turn to something else, if possible, before waking. I—I—"

Here the old gentleman suddenly seized his handkerchief, with a view to wipe his eyes, but, changing his mind, blew his nose instead.

Just then the door opened, and a small domestic entered with that eminently sociable meal, tea. With a final explosion, worthy of Hecla or Vesuvius, the cat shot through the door-way, as if from a catapult, and found refuge in the darkest recesses of the familiar coal-hole.

"But who," said Mr Rigonda, casting his eyes suddenly downward, "who is this charming little brown-eyed maid that you have brought with you from the isles of the southern seas? A native—a little Fiji princess—eh?"

"Hush! father," whispered Pauline in his ear, "she's a dear little orphan who has adopted me as her mother, and would not be persuaded to leave me. So, you see, I've brought her home."

"Quite right, quite right," returned the old man, stooping to kiss the little one. "I've often thought you'd be the better of a sister, Pina, so, perhaps, a daughter will do as well."

"Now, then, tea is ready; draw in your chairs, darlings," said Mrs Rigonda, with a quavering voice. The truth is that all the voices quavered that night, more or less, and it was a matter of uncertainty several times whether the quavering would culminate in laughter or in tears.

"Why do you so often call Pina a queen, dear boy?" asked Mrs Rigonda of her volatile son, Otto.

"Why?" replied the youth, whose excitement did not by any means injure his appetite—to judge from the manner in which he disposed of muffins and toast, sandwiched now and then with wedges of cake—"Why? because she *is* a queen—at least she *was* not long ago."

An incredulous smile playing on the good lady's little mouth, Pauline was obliged to corroborate Otto's statement.

"And what were you queen of?" asked her father, who was plainly under the impression that his children were jesting.

"Of Refuge Islands, daddy," said Pina; "pass the toast, Otto, I think I never *was* so hungry. Coming home obviously improves one's appetite."

"You forget the open boat, Pina."

"Ah, true," returned Pauline, "I did for a moment forget that. Yes, we were fearfully hungry *that* time."

Of course this led to further inquiry, and to Dominick clearing his throat at last, and saying—"Come, I'll give you a short outline of our adventures since we left home. It must only be a mere sketch, of course, because it would take days and weeks to give you all the details."

"Don't be prosy, Dom," said Otto, helping himself to a fifth, if not a tenth, muffin. "Prosiness is one of your weak points when left to your own promptings."

"But before you begin, Dom," said old Mr Rigonda, "tell us where Refuge Islands are."

"In the Southern Pacific, father."

"Yes," observed Otto; "at the bottom of the Southern Pacific."

"Indeed!" exclaimed the old gentleman, whose incredulity was fast taking the form of sarcasm. "Not far, I suppose, from that celebrated island which was the last home and refuge of our famous ancestor, the Spanish pirate, who was distantly related, through a first cousin of his mother, to Don Quixote."

"You doubt us, daddy, I see," said Pauline, laughing; "but I do assure you we are telling you the simple truth. I appeal to Dr Marsh."

Dr Marsh, who had chiefly acted the part of observant listener up to that moment, now assured Mr Rigonda with so much sincerity that what had been told him was true, that he felt bound to believe him.

"Yes, indeed," said Dr Marsh, "your daughter was in truth a queen, and I was one of her subjects. Indeed, I may say that, in one sense, she is a queen still, but she has been dethroned by fire and water, as you shall presently hear, though she still reigns in the affections of her people, and can *never* be dethroned again!"

This speech was greeted with some merriment, for the doctor said it with much enthusiasm. Then Dominick began to give an account of their adventures, interrupted and corrected, not infrequently, by his pert brother Otto, who, being still afflicted with his South-Sea-island appetite, remained unsatisfied until the last slice of toast, and the last muffin, and the last wedge of cake had disappeared from the table.

Dominick's intentions were undoubtedly good; and when he asserted that it was his purpose to give his father and mother merely an outline of their adventures, he was unquestionably sincere; but the outline became so extended, and assumed such a variety of complex convolutions, that there seemed to be no end to the story—as there certainly seemed to be no end to the patience of the listeners. So Dominick went, "on and on and on," as story-books put it, until the fire in the grate began to burn low; until Otto had consumed the contents of the teapot, and the cream-jug, and the sugar-basin, and had even gathered up, economically, the crumbs of the cake; until the still eager audience had begun to yawn considerately with shut mouths; until the household cat, lost in amazement at prolonged neglect, had ventured to creep from the coal-hole, and take up a modest position on the floor, in the shadow of its little old mistress.

There is no saying how long this state of things would have gone on, if it had not been for the exuberant spirits of Otto, who, under an impulse of maternal affection, sprang to his mother's side with intent to embrace her, and unwittingly planted his foot on the cat's tail.

Then, indeed, the convoluted outline came to an abrupt end; for, with a volcanic explosion, suggestive of thunder and lightning, inlaid with dynamite, the hapless creature sprang from the room, followed by a shriek from its mistress, and a roar of laughter from all the rest.

It is not certainly known where that cat spent the following fortnight. The only thing about it that remains on record is the fact that, at the end of that space of time, it returned to its old haunts, deeply humbled, and much reduced; that it gradually became accustomed to the new state of things, and even mounted the table, and sat blinking in its old position, and grew visibly fatter, while the old lady revived old times by stroking it, as she had been wont to, and communicating to it some of her thoughts and fancies.

"Ay, pussy," she said, on one of these occasions when they chanced to be alone together, "little did you and I think, when we used to be sitting so comfortably here, that our darlings were being tossed about and starved in open boats on the stormy sea! Ah! pussy, pussy, we little knew—but 'it's all well that ends well,' as a great writer that you know nothing about has said, and you and I can never, never be thankful enough for getting back, safe and sound, our dear old man, and our darling boys, and our—our little Pauline, the Island Queen."

THE END

Choose from Thousands of 1stWorldLibrary Classics By

A. M. Barnard
Ada Leverson
Adolphus William Ward
Aesop
Agatha Christie
Alexander Aaronsohn
Alexander Kielland
Alexandre Dumas
Alfred Gatty
Alfred Ollivant
Alice Duer Miller
Alice Turner Curtis
Alice Dunbar
Allen Chapman
Alleyne Ireland
Ambrose Bierce
Amelia E. Barr
Amory H. Bradford
Andrew Lang
Andrew McFarland Davis
Andy Adams
Angela Brazil
Anna Alice Chapin
Anna Sewell
Annie Besant
Annie Hamilton Donnell
Annie Payson Call
Annie Roe Carr
Annonaymous
Anton Chekhov
Archibald Lee Fletcher
Arnold Bennett
Arthur C. Benson
Arthur Conan Doyle
Arthur M. Winfield
Arthur Ransome
Arthur Schnitzler
Arthur Train
Atticus
B.H. Baden-Powell
B. M. Bower
B. C. Chatterjee
Baroness Emmuska Orczy
Baroness Orczy
Basil King
Bayard Taylor
Ben Macomber
Bertha Muzzy Bower
Bjornstjerne Bjornson

Booth Tarkington
Boyd Cable
Bram Stoker
C. Collodi
C. E. Orr
C. M. Ingleby
Carolyn Wells
Catherine Parr Traill
Charles A. Eastman
Charles Amory Beach
Charles Dickens
Charles Dudley Warner
Charles Farrar Browne
Charles Ives
Charles Kingsley
Charles Klein
Charles Hanson Towne
Charles Lathrop Pack
Charles Romyn Dake
Charles Whibley
Charles Willing Beale
Charlotte M. Braeme
Charlotte M. Yonge
Charlotte Perkins Stetson
Clair W. Hayes
Clarence Day Jr.
Clarence E. Mulford
Clemence Housman
Confucius
Coningsby Dawson
Cornelis DeWitt Wilcox
Cyril Burleigh
D. H. Lawrence
Daniel Defoe
David Garnett
Dinah Craik
Don Carlos Janes
Donald Keyhoe
Dorothy Kilner
Dougan Clark
Douglas Fairbanks
E. Nesbit
E. P. Roe
E. Phillips Oppenheim
E. S. Brooks
Earl Barnes
Edgar Rice Burroughs
Edith Van Dyne
Edith Wharton

Edward Everett Hale
Edward J. O'Biren
Edward S. Ellis
Edwin L. Arnold
Eleanor Atkins
Eleanor Hallowell Abbott
Eliot Gregory
Elizabeth Gaskell
Elizabeth McCracken
Elizabeth Von Arnim
Ellem Key
Emerson Hough
Emilie F. Carlen
Emily Bronte
Emily Dickinson
Enid Bagnold
Enilor Macartney Lane
Erasmus W. Jones
Ernie Howard Pie
Ethel May Dell
Ethel Turner
Ethel Watts Mumford
Eugene Sue
Eugenie Foa
Eugene Wood
Eustace Hale Ball
Evelyn Everett-green
Everard Cotes
F. H. Cheley
F. J. Cross
F. Marion Crawford
Fannie E. Newberry
Federick Austin Ogg
Ferdinand Ossendowski
Fergus Hume
Florence A. Kilpatrick
Fremont B. Deering
Francis Bacon
Francis Darwin
Frances Hodgson Burnett
Frances Parkinson Keyes
Frank Gee Patchin
Frank Harris
Frank Jewett Mather
Frank L. Packard
Frank V. Webster
Frederic Stewart Isham
Frederick Trevor Hill
Frederick Winslow Taylor

Friedrich Kerst
Friedrich Nietzsche
Fyodor Dostoyevsky
G.A. Henty
G.K. Chesterton
Gabrielle E. Jackson
Garrett P. Serviss
Gaston Leroux
George A. Warren
George Ade
Geroge Bernard Shaw
George Cary Eggleston
George Durston
George Ebers
George Eliot
George Gissing
George MacDonald
George Meredith
George Orwell
George Sylvester Viereck
George Tucker
George W. Cable
George Wharton James
Gertrude Atherton
Gordon Casserly
Grace E. King
Grace Gallatin
Grace Greenwood
Grant Allen
Guillermo A. Sherwell
Gulielma Zollinger
Gustav Flaubert
H. A. Cody
H. B. Irving
H.C. Bailey
H. G. Wells
H. H. Munro
H. Irving Hancock
H. R. Naylor
H. Rider Haggard
H. W. C. Davis
Haldeman Julius
Hall Caine
Hamilton Wright Mabie
Hans Christian Andersen
Harold Avery
Harold McGrath
Harriet Beecher Stowe
Harry Castlemon
Harry Coghill
Harry Houidini

Hayden Carruth
Helent Hunt Jackson
Helen Nicolay
Hendrik Conscience
Hendy David Thoreau
Henri Barbusse
Henrik Ibsen
Henry Adams
Henry Ford
Henry Frost
Henry James
Henry Jones Ford
Henry Seton Merriman
Henry W Longfellow
Herbert A. Giles
Herbert Carter
Herbert N. Casson
Herman Hesse
Hildegard G. Frey
Homer
Honore De Balzac
Horace B. Day
Horace Walpole
Horatio Alger Jr.
Howard Pyle
Howard R. Garis
Hugh Lofting
Hugh Walpole
Humphry Ward
Ian Maclaren
Inez Haynes Gillmore
Irving Bacheller
Isabel Cecilia Williams
Isabel Hornibrook
Israel Abrahams
Ivan Turgenev
J.G.Austin
J. Henri Fabre
J. M. Barrie
J. M. Walsh
J. Macdonald Oxley
J. R. Miller
J. S. Fletcher
J. S. Knowles
J. Storer Clouston
J. W. Duffield
Jack London
Jacob Abbott
James Allen
James Andrews
James Baldwin

James Branch Cabell
James DeMille
James Joyce
James Lane Allen
James Lane Allen
James Oliver Curwood
James Oppenheim
James Otis
James R. Driscoll
Jane Abbott
Jane Austen
Jane L. Stewart
Janet Aldridge
Jens Peter Jacobsen
Jerome K. Jerome
Jessie Graham Flower
John Buchan
John Burroughs
John Cournos
John F. Kennedy
John Gay
John Glasworthy
John Habberton
John Joy Bell
John Kendrick Bangs
John Milton
John Philip Sousa
John Taintor Foote
Jonas Lauritz Idemil Lie
Jonathan Swift
Joseph A. Altsheler
Joseph Carey
Joseph Conrad
Joseph E. Badger Jr
Joseph Hergesheimer
Joseph Jacobs
Jules Vernes
Julian Hawthrone
Julie A Lippmann
Justin Huntly McCarthy
Kakuzo Okakura
Karle Wilson Baker
Kate Chopin
Kenneth Grahame
Kenneth McGaffey
Kate Langley Bosher
Kate Langley Bosher
Katherine Cecil Thurston
Katherine Stokes
L. A. Abbot
L. T. Meade

L. Frank Baum
Latta Griswold
Laura Dent Crane
Laura Lee Hope
Laurence Housman
Lawrence Beasley
Leo Tolstoy
Leonid Andreyev
Lewis Carroll
Lewis Sperry Chafer
Lilian Bell
Lloyd Osbourne
Louis Hughes
Louis Joseph Vance
Louis Tracy
Louisa May Alcott
Lucy Fitch Perkins
Lucy Maud Montgomery
Luther Benson
Lydia Miller Middleton
Lyndon Orr
M. Corvus
M. H. Adams
Margaret E. Sangster
Margret Howth
Margaret Vandercook
Margaret W. Hungerford
Margret Penrose
Maria Edgeworth
Maria Thompson Daviess
Mariano Azuela
Marion Polk Angellotti
Mark Overton
Mark Twain
Mary Austin
Mary Catherine Crowley
Mary Cole
Mary Hastings Bradley
Mary Roberts Rinehart
Mary Rowlandson
M. Wollstonecraft Shelley
Maud Lindsay
Max Beerbohm
Myra Kelly
Nathaniel Hawthrone
Nicolo Machiavelli
O. F. Walton
Oscar Wilde

Owen Johnson
P.G. Wodehouse
Paul and Mabel Thorne
Paul G. Tomlinson
Paul Severing
Percy Brebner
Percy Keese Fitzhugh
Peter B. Kyne
Plato
Quincy Allen
R. Derby Holmes
R. L. Stevenson
R. S. Ball
Rabindranath Tagore
Rahul Alvares
Ralph Bonehill
Ralph Henry Barbour
Ralph Victor
Ralph Waldo Emmerson
Rene Descartes
Ray Cummings
Rex Beach
Rex E. Beach
Richard Harding Davis
Richard Jefferies
Richard Le Gallienne
Robert Barr
Robert Frost
Robert Gordon Anderson
Robert L. Drake
Robert Lansing
Robert Lynd
Robert Michael Ballantyne
Robert W. Chambers
Rosa Nouchette Carey
Rudyard Kipling
Saint Augustine
Samuel B. Allison
Samuel Hopkins Adams
Sarah Bernhardt
Sarah C. Hallowell
Selma Lagerlof
Sherwood Anderson
Sigmund Freud
Standish O'Grady
Stanley Weyman
Stella Benson
Stella M. Francis

Stephen Crane
Stewart Edward White
Stijn Streuvels
Swami Abhedananda
Swami Parmananda
T. S. Ackland
T. S. Arthur
The Princess Der Ling
Thomas A. Janvier
Thomas A Kempis
Thomas Anderton
Thomas Bailey Aldrich
Thomas Bulfinch
Thomas De Quincey
Thomas Dixon
Thomas H. Huxley
Thomas Hardy
Thomas More
Thornton W. Burgess
U. S. Grant
Upton Sinclair
Valentine Williams
Various Authors
Vaughan Kester
Victor Appleton
Victor G. Durham
Victoria Cross
Virginia Woolf
Wadsworth Camp
Walter Camp
Walter Scott
Washington Irving
Wilbur Lawton
Wilkie Collins
Willa Cather
Willard F. Baker
William Dean Howells
William le Queux
W. Makepeace Thackeray
William W. Walter
William Shakespeare
Winston Churchill
Yei Theodora Ozaki
Yogi Ramacharaka
Young E. Allison
Zane Grey

www.ingramcontent.com/pod-product-compliance
Lightning Source LLC
Chambersburg PA
CBHW030307180626
46810CB00003B/953